Conrad Gallagher's

New Irish Cooking

Conrad Gallagher's
New Irish Cooking

Recipes from
Dublin's Peacock Alley

A. & A. Farmar

Editing and additional text by Domini Kemp

Colour photographs by Walter Pfeiffer,
except those on page 97 and the back cover
which are by Brian Daly.
Black and white photographs by Brian Daly.
Cover design by Bluett
Designed and typeset by A. & A. Farmar
Index by Helen Litton
Printed in Ireland by Betaprint

ISBN 1899047 29 8

Acknowledgements

Among the countless people whom I have met in my career, some have influenced me in purely professional ways whilst others have become friends.

I would like to thank the following: from my early days, Seán and Brian McEniff, Tim and Carmel O'Sullivan and all the staff in Renvyle House; in New York: Seán James, Tom Moran, Joe Friel, and especially my brother Keith who encouraged me to go to New York; the chefs from New York whose work especially influenced me: Laurent Manrique, Joe Friel, Jacques Torres, John Doherty and the great Daniel Boulud and the staff from Le Cirque: I would like to thank Laurent Manrique especially for helping me to get the job with Alain Ducasse in Monte Carlo. The standard of perfection constantly achieved in the Hotel de Paris is a goal I strive for constantly in my restaurant. What I learned there is invaluable, and the opportunity to work with one of the best chefs in the world is an experience I will always treasure.

When I was starting up my own restaurant: I will always be thankful for the support, advice and friendship of those whose expertise in various fields has helped me along the way, Tony Campbell, Lorraine Hayes, Frank Ennis, Roddy Comyn, Brendan Malone, Conrad Lyons, Michael Hickey, Gerry Kane, Geoff Simpson, Jerry Reddin, and Gerry McGurn. Although intense competition means that restaurateurs rarely make the transition from competitors to close friends, I am lucky enough to be able to consider Derry and Sally Ann Clarke, Ross Lewis, and Robbie and Shirley Millar, good friends.

Restaurant critics and food writers can be the bane of a restaurateur's life but I would like to thank the following for their continuing praise of Peacock Alley: Vincent Jamison, Sally and John McKenna, Tom Doorley, Nell Stewart Liberty and Petra Carter. I would also like to thank Brian Waddell, Siobhán O'Gorman and all the team at 'Gourmet Ireland' and Paul and Jeanne Rankin for their support.

Restaurants cannot survive without a good team behind them. I have been lucky enough to have had some wonderfully talented chefs and floor staff work for me, including Sharon Hollywood, Gavin O'Rourke, Johnny Aitken, Brian Beattie, Nick Meunier, Brendan Geoghegan, Rory Gethin, Denise MacBrien and Kevin Watson to name but a few. Thanks also to Paul Kelly who helped test all the recipes, and Peaches Taaffe who kindly let us take over her kitchen for two weeks whilst all the recipe-testing was being done. Thanks also to Dr John Armstrong and Dr Michael Butler who helped me through the cancer, and for their wonderful post operative care.

Thank you to Walter Pfeiffer and Brian Daly for the superb photography, Vincent Jamison for his excellent wine notes and writing, and Tony and Anna Farmar for not only being wonderful publishers, but also so full of encouragement when we couldn't see the end in sight! Also thanks to Linda Kenny and Viv Gaine for the PR. Special thanks to my parents, Evelyn and Michael Gallagher, my uncle Frank Monaghan and all the rest of my family, friends and brilliant customers whose praise and loyalty make the whole job worthwhile.

Finally, and most importantly, thanks to Domini, my sharpest critic and greatest supporter, who devoted countless hours to this book, and transformed it from the original idea into a reality.

Conrad Gallagher
Peacock Alley
October 1997

Contents

Wine Suggestions with the Recipes

by Vincent Jamison

To Domini—

the key person in this

as in everything else.

A Modernist in the Kitchen

Conrad Gallagher is helping to create a renaissance in Irish cooking. He is developing a modernist cuisine in a country where modernism arrived quite early in literature and the visual arts, but very late in the kitchen. Traditionalists do not necessarily like him for this, but they have to admire his consistency and his talent. He does not adhere to the traditionalist assumption that cooking is primarily about simplicity, or that flavours should be restricted to two or three on the plate. Above all, he has no sympathy for the view that the diner should never be assaulted by complex dishes. In the end, Gallagher follows his instincts, which have given him a profound conviction that he can be the best at what he does. In that respect, his mentors are the modern Irish writers and artists—the Wildes and Joyces and Becketts—all of whom dealt with the petty criticism that their work was ambitious and over-the-top.

But if Conrad Gallagher is not a traditionalist, it would be a mistake to assume that he has not had a traditional training. He has had more professional training than any Irish chef of his age. He has graduated from cooking college and has worked in some of the world's greatest kitchens. He was a star in New York at the age of twenty-two; by twenty-four, he had his own successful restaurant in Dublin; and by twenty-five he had moved to a larger and even more successful room.

Why then, do so many traditionalists not like a chef who would seem to have followed a classic career path? Perhaps it is precisely because they see him as a destroyer of all that is simple and uncomplicated in the 'basics' of the Irish kitchen. One way to illustrate this is to take a dish which would traditionally call for a straightforward festive style of cooking—the sort of recipe that might have been handed down in a family—and to give it a treatment that is distinctive, powerful and modern. Gallagher's roasted chestnut soup with duck rillettes is a rare experience—rillettes presented at the bottom of an empty soup bowl, into which is ladled at the table a thick and creamy broth made from the chestnuts, a stock of pheasant and a greatly reduced Madeira. There is actually very little cream in the soup, but the intensity of flavour and suppleness make it as creamy and intense as a great white Burgundy.

Gallagher is capable of other stunningly well-conceived soups, all of which offer a concentration of flavour that is almost startling. Again, soup is a bastion of traditional cooking and many who regard themselves as experts will insist that a particular recipe must be followed. Gallagher however is not afraid to bring in other influences: there is for example, his consommé of tomato and pepper with red pepper capellini. This is, if you like, a version of that most basic of haute cuisine soups—the beef consommé. But it is what a gifted chef does to consommé that transforms it, not the fact that the classic recipe is followed.

Gallagher will also serve starters like crabmeat salad with lemon and beetroot or roast quail breast with pumpkin risotto and mango and coriander salsa. He may follow this with pan-seared bass with fennel purée, fennel confit, spiced lentils and bouillabaisse sauce. This main dish is a visual triumph, piled high and layered in a style that his detractors love to hate—but which is a marvellous trompe l'oeil for those who are not biased in this regard.

Much of Conrad Gallagher's cooking pays homage to Mediterranean and Pacific cuisine, but it also reflects an international style that is itself an indication of how Dublin is turning its face outwards, and in doing so is slowly shaking off the influences of the Pale, of the Ascendancy 'Big Houses', and of its own Victorian 'villages'. The rest of Ireland is following—and sometimes indeed the periphery is leading the centre.

Gallagher, of course, is a man of the periphery himself, and just as the cooking of Lyon or Dordogne has challenged the hegemony of Paris, so Irish regional cooking represents an irreverent challenge to the old Anglo-Irish cooking of the centre—and also to the assumption that Irish cuisine is at its best in country houses, or in regional 'schools' of gastronomy such as Ballymaloe.

The difference between Gallagher's cooking and that of many of his traditionalist contemporaries is that while most Irish chefs are content to let the produce of land and sea speak for itself, chefs like Gallagher are more like artists or architects or fashion designers, who do not simply cook but also design and build food on a plate. The produce itself, and the technical facility in dealing with it, is important but so is the act of creation. And if, in some cases, the patrons are puzzled by what they see, that is nothing new in the history of any culture, or any form of creation. The artists of the Renaissance were just as much a puzzle to the patrons and popes who commissioned their work. So while a chef like Gallagher depends upon the patronage of his customers, he has a more visionary view of what he is doing than a mere offering of service in pursuit of money or a cult following.

The Making of a Chef

Some people are born to music or mathematics, some to calculus or celibacy. Conrad Gallagher was born to cook. He learned baking and basic cooking skills in his mother Evelyn's kitchen in Donegal, that harshly beautiful county of bogland and mountains, bounded to the west and north by the Atlantic. It is a county where traditions linger, where a strong Gaelic-speaking tradition is retained, and where for centuries young men left whitewashed cottages to find seasonal work in Scotland, or in the industrial cities of North America. Many did not return. At seventeen, Conrad Gallagher was younger than most when he left for New York; and he was younger than most when he returned, via France, to dazzle the Dublin restaurant scene with innovative cooking.

Three years after returning to Ireland, Conrad Gallagher owned a distinguished eighty-seater Dublin restaurant, Peacock Alley. He had just turned twenty-six, and already he had spent half of his working life in the kitchen. And if the formative kitchen was his mother's, his professional experience had embraced everything from small-town hotels to the world's leading three-star restaurants.

Conrad is the second-eldest in a family of four. His father Michael worked for the telephone company, Telecom Eireann. Conrad went to local schools in Letterkenny, a quiet inland town where people were more interested in football than in restaurants. He was as bored at school as many mercurial spirits tend to be, and by the age of eleven, he was ready for change. During an international car rally weekend in Donegal, a local hotel, Ballyrane Hotel, recruited casual staff, and Conrad got in by telling them he was fifteen. He stayed on to work for them after school and by the summer holidays, he was working full-time—washing dishes, picking a little spinach for the chefs, topping and tailing vegetables, and sweeping out the kitchen. He moved on to preparatory work in the kitchen, then to cooking the classic Irish breakfast of eggs, bacon, sausages, black pudding, tomatoes and toast. By now he was six foot tall and looked a few years older, so it was easier for him to pass himself off as a chef.

But he was not yet a teenager, and although he had little interest in school or in school sports, he was expected to pay more than lip service to the idea of education, which for hundreds of years had been the only escape route from the tyranny of scrabble farming and petty colonialism of the west of Ireland. So Conrad went back to school in September, and worked in the Ballyrane hotel every day after school and at weekends. When he started skipping school on a regular basis, heading off in school uniform on his bicycle to work for the day, his mother inevitably got wind of it through a parent teacher association meeting. At home his father confronted him quietly. 'How is school getting on?' he asked his son, who replied 'Fine' as defiant sons tend to do. 'He kind of understood cooking was what I wanted to do,' says Conrad, 'I tried to explain to him that the only education that I needed was in the kitchen.' He was lucky enough to have parents who were willing to give him his head, but he went back to school for the rest of the year.

By fourteen he was ready to devote himself to the kitchen and soon he was doing virtually everything: assisting with the grill, and preparing starters and desserts. The hotel was taken over and renamed the Mount Errigal, and Conrad was invited to stay on under Seán McEniff.

The following Easter, he was asked to move to a larger sister hotel, the Great Northern, in the seaside resort of Bundoran where

he worked under Brian McEniff. It was here that Conrad learned the fundamentals—how to make béchamel sauce, fillet a plaice, or bone out a sirloin. He had by now become accustomed to working in large cold kitchens, and he had graduated from the traditional Irish breakfast to full lunches and dinners. Hard-pressed chefs at the resort hotel appreciated the help of a resilient and capable young man who could stand in for them during rest periods or days off. He learned a great deal on the job, in what amounted to a traditional apprenticeship, but it would be a mistake to assume that he and other young Irish chefs are merely self-taught. Most have gone to college or catering school. Gallagher had dropped in and out of school, but he needed to formalise his education as a chef—and at fifteen he went to a catering college in the fishing port of Killybegs. He continued to work at weekends at the hotel in Bundoran; and at Easter and in the summer he went to the more stylish Renvyle House in Connemara, a beautiful country house once owned by Oliver St John Gogarty, a prominent figure in James Joyce's novel *Ulysses*. He graduated from Killybegs at seventeen and worked as a *sous chef* that summer in Renvyle. In September he left for New York, where his elder brother was working.

He went to America for work experience, and also to do a diploma in hotel and restaurant management at New York University in Greenwich Village. He had already seen the need to develop the business skills necessary to run his own restaurant. Killybegs had taught him about the more academic and practical aspects of food; Renvyle had taught him the importance of absolutely fresh fish and good local produce; and New York taught him about the restaurant business.

His brother ran a bar in Manhattan. He helped Conrad get a

job as chef at a forty-seater restaurant in Queens called Blue Street. It was so quiet that Conrad had two people for lunch the first day. Within two weeks, however, the word of mouth had gone out and the restaurant was full. One of those who came to eat was a catering manager at the Plaza Hotel, who was surprised to learn that the chef was a seventeen-year-old Irishman. He asked to speak with Conrad, and invited him to do the catering for the christening of one of his children. It helped that the manager's wife was Irish, but the buffet food spoke for itself. The manager suggested that Conrad might like to come in for an interview.

Later, Conrad met the Plaza's executive banqueting chef, Joe Friel, an Irishman who became a good friend. And although he had never even worked in Dublin, he soon found himself in a top New York hotel, alongside a hundred experienced chefs cooking for the high-rollers of Manhattan. He learned new things—how to do a polenta cake with pan-fried breast of mallard duck without allowing a sauce made from duck stock, or a traditional brown sauce, to dominate the dish. He started to educate himself in American cuisine, reading dozens of articles and books. He began at the Plaza as a *chef de partie*, but after two months, he became *chef tournant (sous chef)*.

Gallagher is quick to pay tribute to the way in which Americans run their kitchens: 'Americans are the greatest organisers and managers in the restaurant business.' They are also, he realised, quick to recognise talent. After a year at the Plaza, Gallagher had another fortuitous meeting that let his talent develop in new directions. His brother got him a consultancy fee to help set up a Queens bar-restaurant, but when the chef failed to show up, Conrad and his fellow chefs at the Plaza ran the place in their spare time for the first two weeks. 'We were practising new dishes and it was fun for us all,' says Conrad. The *New York Post* wrote up the brilliant, inexpensive food; and Conrad's brother showed the newspaper write-up to one of the regulars in his Manhattan bar, a food and beverage manager at the Waldorf Astoria hotel. The manager invited Conrad to come in for an interview, and he got a new job under a new chef, Laurent Manrique.

'Manrique was a major influence on me,' says Conrad. 'He is Basque, but he had been in California and had learned the new style. He made me *sous chef* at the gourmet restaurant Peacock Alley. That's where I really learned the basis for my cooking; I learned how to work with everything, from truffles and foie gras to traditional cassoulets.'

At Peacock Alley, Gallagher taught himself Pacific Rim cooking. He developed a gift for using strong, clear flavours—for example, fresh coriander with the Waldorf Astoria crabcake he was later to bring back to Ireland with him. These were deep-fried crabcakes, served with a pungent Basque-style pepper stew. The crab and the pepper stew might seem incompatible to some; that is what Gallagher's cooking is about. He learned how to challenge the palate, how to give the discerning restaurant patron something far removed from home cooking or comfort food. Inevitably, it would lead to a criticism that his food was not 'plain' enough. But celebrities like Bruce Willis, Demi Moore and Melanie Griffith loved it. He appeared on the Robin Leach television programme about the rich and famous. And in 1994 he acted as food consultant to President Bill Clinton's White House for its St Patrick's Day celebration dinner. (The plaque from Clinton thanking him is still on his restaurant wall.)

But just when Gallagher appeared to have conquered the American kitchen, he decided to uproot himself again and head back to

Europe. He wanted to go to the source for a rethink on classical French cuisine, in particular to look at the interface between the traditional haute cuisine of Escoffier, and the nouvelle cuisine of the younger French chefs. He hoped to work with Alain Ducasse, one of the world's greatest chefs. But there was a two-year wait to do a *stage* (a training period) at Ducasse's three-star Michelin restaurant in the Hotel de Paris in Monte Carlo. Fortunately, Leonard Manrique knew Ducasse and got him a place.

Gallagher spent a year with Ducasse, using up his savings in the unpaid training position. He spoke no French and hardly anyone else in the kitchen spoke English. He learned that he was one of the first non-French speakers to work in the hotel in its eighteen-year history. 'It was like being in the army,' says Gallagher. 'You spent half of your day cooking and the other half cleaning. Everything was spotless. They wanted perfection in everything.' Gallagher learned a great deal about the discipline of cooking from Ducasse, who has since opened a major new restaurant in Paris—in the hope, some believe, of becoming the first six-star Michelin chef. For French chefs, getting three stars is everything—and it requires not only brilliant cooking, but impeccable standards of service, good restaurant management, the freshest produce, and the best quality control. After a year, Gallagher was ready to move on with some of the new discipline he had learned. He had used up most of his savings, it was close to Christmas, and he wanted to see his family in Ireland. He left France with the intention of returning however, and he still intends to spend summer holidays, where possible, doing a *stage* with Ducasse.

After a Christmas in Letterkenny, Gallagher headed for Dublin. He took a job as head chef at a small restaurant, Morels in Dún Laoghaire. He stayed only four months, but in that time he turned the small restaurant into one of the hottest spots in town. He did things like pumpkin risotto with black trumpet mushrooms and mascarpone cheese. People loved it, but behind the scenes, the discipline and quest for perfectionism he had learned from Ducasse resulted in him going through six chefs in as many weeks. 'I don't care,' he says, 'there is no room for people who watch the clock in my kitchen.' He also gave suppliers a hard time. 'I had to import the wild duck from France and I'd already been through three meat suppliers and three fish suppliers in five weeks.'

He was biding his time to open his own place, and the opportunity came when another leading chef, Derry Clarke, moved his successful L'Ecrivain restaurant to a larger room. Gallagher took over Clarke's basement room in Lower Baggot Street in Central Dublin. Many of Morels' customers came with him. He called it Peacock Alley after the Waldorf Astoria room, and he announced his intention to do Mediterranean food with the freshest ingredients. He put some of his signature dishes on the menu—daube of ox cheek with roast shallots and morel cream cooked slowly as in pot roasting; he also did pastrami-style salmon and ravioli stuffed with langoustines. Soon, the 40-seater was packed for lunch and dinner.

Inevitably he needed a bigger place. And eleven months after he had opened, he learned of a building on South William Street, closer to the centre of Dublin. He heard on a Monday morning that it might be available, saw it later that day and came back with his accountant to discuss taking over the lease. He went back to cook lunch, then returned at four for serious negotiations. They went on until early in the morning and the deal was signed the next day. Serious renovations began, while Gallagher kept going back to the basement restaurant to keep about one

hundred patrons a day happy. On a Saturday night, two weeks after he had enquired about the building, he closed the basement restaurant, moved the kitchen overnight to the new location, and completed the refit and renovations for opening the following Tuesday.

The new Peacock Alley proved to be a sparkling room, with a large cathedral-roof skylight to give it elevation. It had modern Irish art on the walls (including a painting bought by his grandmother) and a huge copper coffee machine. Conrad had very little capital and no bank support, but he managed to do a major kitchen refit, with stainless steel surfaces everywhere; he also got top quality French glassware, plates and table linen for the dining room. The place looked good, and the food looked better. He now had the kind of room, and the kind of cooking, that would win awards—or it would when the guidebooks got up to speed with his turbo-charged, inventive cooking.

As so often happens, word of mouth moved far faster than the guides. Soon, Gallagher was turning over more than a hundred covers a night. Many visitors were from out of town, or people dining out for a special occasion. In time, Gallagher would need to address the problem that is almost universal in the restaurant business—the problem of repeat business and customer loyalty, which sometimes must be built by encouraging people to eat out more often, perhaps with only one or two courses and for less money than a full-blown *prix fixe* dinner.

Before he could resolve that fully, a much more serious problem arose. He was not yet twenty-six. The restaurant was full for lunch and dinner throughout the busy autumn and winter period leading up to Christmas. Yet he was battling with testicular cancer. For a straight seventy-five days, he had intensive treatment to control the cancer. He kept cooking right through it, except for a Christmas break in Donegal. And by the new year, the cancer was conquered and he was back at work.

Later that year he got engaged to Domini Kemp, proposing to her at Marco-Pierre White's three-star restaurant in London. Domini had grown up in Nassau in the Bahamas, but her father died when she was ten, and the children moved to Ireland with their mother, who is Irish. She went to school in Ireland, and later helped her sister, Peaches Taaffe, in a catering business. Domini also developed her skills in show-jumping and began competing. She opened a tack shop, Sporthorse International, but her showjumping took her to England to compete more actively in international showjumping events. She took a food and wine diploma with Leith's in London. Then, on a visit to Dublin, she met Conrad by chance in the restaurant. Their relationship flourished. As Conrad's partner, she has been invaluable in helping him in the business, taking over the front-of-house operations and helping him expand into new areas. In the catering side of the business, they sold their bread, salad dressing, oils and marinades to major shops and delicatessens.

The restaurant went from strength to strength. But Conrad remained a little dissatisfied with his special occasion reputation. And when another summer came round, with the gospel of lighter eating gaining momentum, he decided to cut his prices and offer people the choice of a single course and a glass of wine. And in a city where most restaurants close on Sunday and sometimes Monday, he decided to go to a seven-day operation, with a special brunch on Sunday.

He already needed about twenty-five people to run the restaurant, but at least his growing reputation meant that young people were continually applying for work. The young tyro was becoming the experienced executive. Young people called him 'Chef' in the kitchen. And indeed he had become something of an archetype for the generations of young Irish who had gone abroad to learn a business, and who for the first time were returning in substantial numbers, so that the country was beginning to have net immigration.

In the kitchens of Ireland, the returned travellers showed off a new style of cooking. Young chefs like Gallagher had roamed the world, bringing home recipes for everything from harissa, a North African chilli jam, to mango and coriander salsa, to wasabi crème fraîche. In the decade from the mid-1980s, the renaissance in Irish cooking was so profound that an experienced English chef and competition judge, Michael Truelove, who had himself held two Michelin stars, could report that the Irish chefs were better than their counterparts in Britain. 'The Irish boys have travelled more and have absorbed all the best influences,' he said simply.

Like many of the leading Irish chefs, Conrad Gallagher's achievement is not just a product of luck, or even of the sea-change in eating habits. The best young chefs have worked hard on every continent to build up the discipline required to create an international cuisine that is neither hackneyed nor merely eclectic: it is a genuine expression of the Irish love of travel, of learning and of richness of expression. Their spiritual mentors in this are not necessarily previous generations of chefs, many of whom trained in the traditional Anglo-Saxon school of 'Big House' cooking, but the Irish artists—in particular the writers—who travelled widely throughout the twentieth century, absorbing the influences of many cultures and languages, and using them to forge a new Irish style.

That style is still emerging. But Conrad Gallagher is its leading exponent, and his expansion plans are likely to stamp his influence on Irish cooking for many years to come. A new one hundred and forty-seater bistro, Lloyds, promises a lighter and less expensive style of cooking in a key central location, opposite Government Buildings and beside Dublin's most distinguished hotel, the Merrion. There, Conrad is setting out to take the distinctive style of Peacock Alley to a broader audience. 'I've had a lot of feedback since I opened,' said Conrad, following a highly successful appearance on the top-rated Late Late Show on television. 'I can serve things like salmon on brown bread or a nice ravioli of lobster. But I need more space and manpower to do what I want to do.' What he is referring to is the success of very large restaurants in New York, London and Paris, where economies of scale can be made to work effectively. Soon enough, Conrad Gallagher will open the really big food hall he needs to display his talents. By then, he will have demonstrated clearly that he is leading Irish cooking into the modernist era, and helping to bring about a renaissance that is as much about the changing nature of culture as it is about cuisine.

SOUPS

Red Pepper and Tomato Consommé with Red Pepper Capellini

Vegetarians love the smoky flavour of this consommé.

The most time-consuming part of this recipe is preparing the to-matoes and red peppers, but the consommé is so delicious that it is well worth the effort.

Method

In a large saucepan, sweat the shallots in the olive oil until soft and transparent. Add 800 g of the red peppers and 2 kg of the tomatoes, reserving the rest for the garnish. Cook for a few minutes, then add the garlic, thyme, peppercorns and sugar. Cover and cook gently for a further 5–10 minutes. Add the water and half the tomato purée. Simmer for 15 minutes. Remove from the heat and allow to cool for an hour.

Sieve into a clean saucepan and, using the back of a ladle, press the pulp through the sieve to extract all the juices. Discard the leftover pulp, season the soup and leave to cool.

To clarify the soup, lightly whisk the egg whites with the basil, parsley and remaining tomato purée, add to the soup and return to a gentle heat. Whisk the mixture for 5–10 minutes, then simmer it very gently for about 30 minutes. A crust should have formed on the surface. Do not break this up by stirring or boiling the liquid.

Using a metal spoon, remove as much of the crust as possible and discard. Line a colander with kitchen paper, muslin, or a clean tea towel. Place over a clean glass bowl, and drain the soup into the bowl. Your consommé should now be clear.

To serve

Reheat the consommé. Season lightly to taste. Blanch the cappellini in boiling water for 3–4 minutes until *al dente*. Drain and place in the bottom of the soup bowls along with the remaining red peppers and tomatoes. Ladle the consommé on to the cappellini and sprinkle some sliced basil into each bowl. Serve immediately.

Serves 4

8 shallots, peeled and finely chopped
200 ml olive oil
1 kg red peppers, roasted and chopped (see page 128)
2.5 kg overnight baked tomatoes (see page 127)
8 cloves garlic, peeled and crushed
12 sprigs thyme
2 teaspoons black peppercorns
2 tablespoons sugar
2 litres water
2 tablespoons tomato purée
6 egg whites
1 bunch basil, chopped
1 bunch parsley, chopped
salt and freshly ground black pepper

Garnishes

200 g red pepper capellini (see page 113)
1 tablespoon basil, finely sliced

Tomato and Basil Soup with Vermicelli Baskets and Goats' Cheese Guacamole

The delicate flavour of this soup is reflected in its pale colour.

For even more flavour, use half vine-ripened tomatoes and half overnight baked tomatoes (see page 127). The colour of the soup is quite pale, with a delicate tomato flavour. It is worth making the guacamole. If you leave out the other garnishes, just spoon a quenelle of guacamole on top of the soup before serving.

Method

In a large saucepan sweat the olive oil, shallots, garlic and thyme, without allowing the vegetables to colour. After 3–4 minutes, add the tomato halves and sauté for another 2–3 minutes. Season with salt and pepper.

Reduce the heat and add the lemon grass and tomato purée. Stir occasionally and cook gently for a further 10–12 minutes, taking care that the mixture does not burn.

Add the chicken stock and turn up the heat. Simmer for 20–30 minutes. Reduce the heat and add the Parmesan, cream and half the basil leaves. Cook for a further 5 minutes and then remove from the heat. Remove the lemon grass and allow to cool slightly before processing in a blender or food processor. Pass through a fine sieve and discard any pulp remaining in the sieve (for an extra-smooth texture, sieve once again). Adjust the seasoning.

To serve

Slice the remaining basil into very fine strips and add it to the soup with the chervil. Place a vermicelli basket in the centre of each bowl, and a quenelle of the guacamole into each basket. Place a deep-fried basil leaf in each quenelle of guacamole and drizzle each bowl with some tomato oil.

Gently ladle some soup into the bowl and serve immediately.

Serves 4
80 ml olive oil
3 shallots, peeled and chopped
6 cloves garlic, peeled and chopped
3 sprigs of thyme
5 kg vine-ripened plum tomatoes, skinned, seeded and halved
salt and freshly ground black pepper
1 stalk lemon grass
50 ml tomato purée
800 ml chicken stock (see page 166)
75 g Parmesan, grated
80 ml cream
100 g basil leaves
1 tablespoon chervil, chopped

Garnishes

1 recipe vermicelli baskets (see page 30)
½ recipe goats' cheese guacamole (see page 30)
4 deep-fried basil leaves (see page 128)
40 ml tomato oil (see page 169)

Vermicelli Baskets

Use these mini baskets to garnish your favourite soups. Fill with anything from fondue of tomato to goats' cheese guacamole.

Method

Arrange a quarter of the pasta around the inside of a small ladle to make a basket shape, cover with another ladle to keep the shape and deep fry in vegetable oil, using both ladles, at 170°C/325°F until golden brown.

Drain on kitchen paper and season with salt. Repeat with the remaining pasta. Use immediately or allow to cool fully, then store in an airtight container and reheat in a warm oven.

Makes 4 small baskets
100 g vermicelli, cooked
vegetable oil
salt

Goats' Cheese Guacamole

This is best made as close to serving as possible. However, if you need to make it a few hours in advance, pour a layer of lemon or lime juice over the top of the guacamole. This will prevent the avocados from becoming too discoloured. Pour off the excess juice and mix well before serving.

Method

Cut the avocados in half and remove the stones. Scoop out the flesh and place in a food processor or blender with the other ingredients.

Process until smooth then pass the mixture through a fine sieve. If you are using beautifully ripe avocados it is not necessary to sieve. Adjust the seasoning and chill until ready to use. Use within a few hours.

Serves 4
2 avocados
25 g goats' cheese, rind removed, chopped
juice of 1 lime or 1 small lemon
1 tablespoon coriander, finely chopped
salt and freshly ground black pepper

Corn Soup with Oysters, Roasted Peppers and Smoked Chilli Butter

A rich and buttery soup beautifully complemented by the oysters

The oysters are optional, but are a lovely touch for a special occasion. They are not cooked in this recipe, but the soup will heat them. Oysters are best served at temperatures not exceeding 80°C/175°F.

Method
Heat the olive oil in a large saucepan. Sweat the shallots and garlic in the olive oil, but do not allow them to colour.

Add the butter, rosemary, corn kernels, a total of 750 ml of corn liquor and/or stock, bring to the boil, then reduce the heat and simmer for 10 minutes. Add the cream, bring back to the boil, reduce the heat again and simmer for another 15 minutes. Season with salt and pepper.

Allow to cool and blend in a food processor. Pass through a sieve and return to a clean saucepan. Adjust seasoning and reheat as necessary.

To serve
Carefully remove the oysters from the shells and rinse in a bowl of salted water. Arrange the rocket leaves and roasted peppers in the base of the soup bowls. Unwrap the butter and slice into thin rounds. Put two rounds into each bowl and place an oyster on top. Gently ladle the soup into each bowl. Serve immediately.

Serves 4
1 tablespoon olive oil
2 shallots, peeled and chopped
6 cloves garlic, peeled and crushed
25 g butter
1 sprig rosemary
1 recipe braised corn (see page 32)
750 ml chicken or vegetable stock (see page 166/7)
250 ml cream
salt and freshly ground white pepper

Garnishes
4 oysters
8 rocket leaves
1 recipe roasted red peppers (see page 128)
½ recipe smoked chilli butter (see page 32)

Braised Corn

Braising corn is a great way of bringing out all its flavour without overcooking it. In Peacock Alley we use only fresh corn on the cob, but if you can't get it, you can use frozen corn on the cob. The taste won't be as good, but providing your stock is good enough, probably no one except you will know the difference.

Method

Preheat the oven to 160°C/325°F/gas mark 3.

Place all the ingredients into an ovenproof dish, cover and braise for about 45 minutes, turning the cobs occasionally.

Remove the cobs from the dish, strain the liquid into a bowl and reserve. Scrape the kernels into a bowl and set aside until required.

Serves 4

4 corn on the cob
300 ml chicken stock or vegetable stock (see page 166/7)
2 sprigs rosemary
30 g butter
5 shallots, peeled and chopped
6 cloves garlic, peeled and chopped

Smoked Chilli Butter

Chilli butter can also be used to flavour risottos, polenta, couscous, pasta, etc.

Method

Mix the butter with the other ingredients until they are all well incorporated. Lay out a sheet of clingfilm and place the butter on the clingfilm in the shape of a log or sausage. Roll up the clingfilm and secure the ends.

To get a smoother sausage shape, use several layers of clingfilm. Chill until ready to serve. Keeps for 2–3 days.

125 g butter, softened
25 g dried chillies, diced
65 g smoked chillies, diced
15 g ginger, peeled and chopped
15 g coriander, chopped
salt and freshly ground black pepper

Corn Soup with Oysters, Roasted Peppers and Smoked Chilli Butter

[33]

Pumpkin Soup with Crème Fraîche and Rocket

The slightly sweet flavour is balanced by the tartness of the rocket leaves and crème fraîche.

Pumpkins are very popular in Northern France and North America. In the United States they are used for filling for sweet pumpkin pies whereas in France they are used in savoury pies. We use the seeds as garnish for soup, but they could also be substituted for pine nuts to make a pumpkin seed pesto.

Method

Quarter the pumpkin. Remove the seeds and toast them lightly under the grill. Reserve for the garnish. Remove the fibre and cut off the skin, then cut the pumpkin flesh into 1 cm cubes.

Heat the olive oil in a large saucepan and sweat the diced pumpkin, shallots, garlic and thyme for 5 minutes. Season well and cook gently for about a further 10 minutes, but do not allow the mixture to take on any colour.

Increase the heat and gradually add the chicken stock. Adding the stock gradually rather than all at once allows the liquid to reduce a little and intensifies the flavour.

Simmer for 20–30 minutes, then add half the Parmesan, all the cream and 1 tablespoon of crème fraîche.

Cook for another 5 minutes, then remove from the heat and allow to cool slightly before processing in a blender or food processor. Pass the soup through a fine sieve into a clean saucepan. Using the back of a small ladle, press down the pulp to extract the juices. Discard any remaining pulp. Adjust the seasoning and reheat as necessary.

To serve

Place quennelles of crème fraîche and some pumpkin seeds in the base of each bowl and gently ladle soup on top. Serve immediately.

Serves 4

1 large pumpkin, 2–3 kg to yield 750 g pumpkin flesh
100 ml olive oil
3 shallots, peeled and chopped
3 cloves garlic, peeled and finely chopped
2 tablespoons thyme, finely chopped
salt and freshly ground black pepper
1 litre chicken or vegetable stock (see page 166/7)
50 g Parmesan, shaved
100 ml cream
1 tablespoon crème fraîche

Garnishes

2 tablespoons crème fraîche
12 rocket leaves
toasted pumpkin seeds

Roast Chestnut Soup with Duck Rillettes

The intensity of flavour and suppleness make this soup as creamy and powerful as a great white Burgundy.

This soup is very rich. The amount given below may seem quite small, but when served with the garnish, it is more than adequate as a starter. Chestnuts are extremely nutritious and full of starch so be careful not to overblend in the food processor or the starch will start to overwork.

Method

Heat the olive oil in a large saucepan and sweat the shallots and garlic for 3 minutes. Add the rosemary, sage and thyme and cook for another minute. Add the chestnuts and cook for a further 2 minutes.

Add the Madeira and increase the heat slightly so that the Madeira reduces by at least half. Add the butter and gradually add the stock. Simmer gently for 20–25 minutes.

Add the cream and season with salt and pepper. Remove from the heat and allow to cool slightly before placing in a blender or food processor. Purée until smooth and pass through a sieve into a saucepan. Using the back of a ladle, push the chestnut pulp through the sieve. Discard any remaining.

Adjust the seasoning if necessary, or allow to cool fully and reheat as required.

To serve

Place quenelles of the duck rillettes into each bowl and gently ladle in the soup. Serve immediately.

Serves 4
50 ml olive oil
3 shallots, peeled and finely chopped
3 cloves garlic, peeled and chopped
2 sprigs rosemary
2 sage leaves
2 sprigs thyme
900 g peeled chestnuts
50 ml Madeira
50 g butter
1 litre chicken stock (see page 166)
150 ml cream
salt and freshly ground black pepper

Garnish
½ recipe duck rillettes (see page 36)

Duck Rillettes

Rillettes are best described as coarse patés. In this recipe the duck is braised and then processed with a little cooking liquor and some prunes that have been soaked overnight in Armagnac. In Peacock Alley we enrich the rillettes further by adding some seared foie gras or trimmings from a foie gras terrine before processing. We use it for canapés, in soup, and as stuffing for ravioli.

50g prunes, stoned
50 ml Armagnac
4 duck legs
salt and freshly ground black pepper
1 tablespoon olive oil
30 g butter
3 cloves garlic, peeled and crushed
2 sprigs thyme
4 shallots, peeled and roughly chopped
1 litre chicken stock (see page 166)
30 g butter, melted

Method

Soak the prunes in the Armagnac overnight. (If you forget to soak the prunes, just heat them in a small saucepan with the Armagnac over a very gentle heat for a few minutes, and then allow them to marinate while the duck is cooking.)

Preheat the oven to 150°C/300°F/gas mark 2.

Season the duck legs with salt and freshly ground black pepper. Heat the olive oil in a large frying pan, and sear the duck legs on all sides until well browned. Add the butter, garlic, thyme and shallots. Cook for another minute and then gradually add enough chicken stock to deglaze the pan. Transfer everything to an ovenproof dish. Add the remaining chicken stock. The duck legs should be covered in liquid.

Cook for 1½ hours and then check the duck legs. The meat should be falling away from the bone. If not, cook for another half hour. Remove from the oven and allow the duck legs to cool in the cooking liquor.

When they are cool enough to handle, tear the meat away from the bone and place in a food processor, along with the soaked prunes. Process until smooth, adding some of the cooking liquor and a little of the melted butter to help bind the mixture. You may not need to add any butter, it all depends on how fatty the duck is. Season and refrigerate until ready to use.

To serve hot, simply heat the rillettes in a saucepan with some extra butter.

STARTERS

Pastrami-style Salmon with Japanese Rice, Pickled Ginger, Pear and Cucumber with Wasabi Crème Fraîche

Double marination of salmon produces subtle flavours balanced by pickled ginger and other ingredients, not unlike well-made sushi.

For this recipe the salmon undergoes two separate cures, each lasting 24 hours. It will then keep for two days if refrigerated and well wrapped. Prepare all the garnishes well in advance, so that all you have to do is decorate the plates and serve.

Method
Skin the salmon, run your fingers against the grain of the flesh and remove the pin bones with tweezers.

Place the coriander seeds on a baking tray and toast under the grill for a few minutes. Allow to cool and then crush.

Mix all the ingredients for the first marinade together. Lay out a double layer of clingfilm at least twice the size of the salmon and place half the marinade on one half of the clingfilm. Place the salmon on top and then spread the remaining marinade on top of the salmon. Wrap well with clingfilm and refrigerate for 24 hours. Next day, unwrap the salmon and scrape off and discard the first marinade.

Mix together the ingredients for the second marinade. Lay out the clingfilm as before and smear the top of the salmon with the second marinade. Place the smeared side of the salmon down on the clingfilm and smear the other side. Wrap tightly in the clingfilm and refrigerate for a further 24 hours.

Melt the butter in a saucepan and cook the rice for a minute or until well coated with butter. Add a few tablespoons of stock or water and continue to stir until the liquid becomes absorbed.

Repeat this process of adding stock or water gradually for about 15 minutes or until the rice is cooked. Spread the rice out on a baking sheet to cool and then shape into quenelles. Refrigerate until ready to use.

Sprinkle 2 tablespoons of lemon juice on the diced cucumber and pear. Mix the crème fraîche, wasabi and the remaining lemon juice.

Serves 4
360 g salmon fillet

First marinade
1 tablespoon coriander seeds
60 g coarse sea salt
juice and rind from ½ orange
juice and rind from ½ lemon
freshly ground black pepper

Second marinade
2 tablespoons Dijon mustard
1 teaspoon dill, finely chopped
1 teaspoon lemon balm, finely chopped
1 teaspoon coriander, finely chopped
1 teaspoon chervil, finely chopped

20 g butter
150 g Japanese rice
300 ml chicken or vegetable stock or water
juice of 2 lemons
½ cucumber, finely diced
1 pear, peeled and finely diced
50 g crème fraîche
½ teaspoon wasabi
4 radishes, finely sliced
1 recipe pickled ginger (see page 39)
2 tablespoons dill oil (see page 168)
chives
2 chives, chopped into 2 cm lengths
1 bunch dill

To serve

Remove the salmon from the fridge and slice as thinly as possible. Arrange a few slices in the centre of each plate. Spoon some pear and cucumber around the edge of the plate. Dot some wasabi crème fraîche in between the cucumber and pear. Place a radish slice beside the pear and the pickled ginger beside the radish. Drizzle some dill oil on the plate and place a quenelle of rice on the salmon. Stick the chives in the crème fraîche, and garnish with the dill.

Pickled Ginger

Ginger is extremely versatile being used to flavour foods from ginger beer to cakes, jams, meat, tea, curries and marinades. Pickled ginger is available from Asian markets and is quite suitable for the salmon dish. It looks different from the pickled ginger here which is beige/brown in colour and quite coarse.

Serves 4
½ leek, white part only, chopped
½ onion, peeled and chopped
1 celery stick, chopped
1 garlic clove, peeled and crushed
150 ml white wine
1 tablespoon olive oil
75 ml white wine vinegar
1 tablespoon sugar
sprig of thyme
½ stalk lemon grass
8 cm piece root ginger, peeled and very finely sliced
salt and freshly ground white pepper

Method

Soak the leek, onion, celery and garlic in the white wine overnight. Drain, reserving the wine. Heat the olive oil and sauté the marinated vegetables for a few minutes. Remove from the oil with a slotted spoon and place in a saucepan with the reserved wine, white wine vinegar and sugar. Bring to the boil and add the thyme, lemongrass and ginger. Cover and simmer very gently for an hour.

Remove the ginger with a slotted spoon and set aside. Remove and discard the thyme and lemongrass. Allow the pickling juice to cool, add the ginger and season with salt and pepper. It will keep in a sealed jar in the refrigerator for up to a week.

Wine Suggestion

Spicy Japanese elements, particularly pickled ginger and wasabi, make for a difficult match with wine. A small bottle of saki, warmed in a container of warm water, will do as well as anything. Another good white wine choice is viognier, preferably a Condrieu from the northern Rhône. The best viognier has a creamy, floral waxiness, with a touch of apricots and peaches, which will help it wrap around the crème fraîche without overwhelming the salmon. There are some good New World viogniers, and the grape also works well in blends with roussane, marsanne and other varietals. In blends, it is particularly good at adding an attractive fragrance and roundness to thin white wines, which would be wrong with this dish.

Roast Quail Breast with Pumpkin Risotto and Mango and Coriander Salsa

Roast Quail Breast with Pumpkin Risotto and Mango and Coriander Salsa

Delicate but supple little quail breasts add a touch of gaminess to complex fruity flavours of pumpkin and a mango salsa

This is a fairly simple recipe but looks very impressive when served, with great contrasting flavours and textures. The quail cooks very quickly and you can prepare everything else ahead of time. The risotto can be half cooked, the prepared leek and carrot will only take a minute to cook, and the salsa can be made the night before.

Serves 4

4 quail
salt and freshly ground black pepper
1 tablespoon olive oil
1 recipe pumpkin risotto, prepared in advance (see page 115)
1 leek, finely sliced into julienne strips
1 carrot, peeled and finely sliced into strips
30 g butter
1 small bunch chopped chives
1 recipe mango and coriander salsa (see below)

Garnishes

4 vanilla pods
4 Parmesan shavings
12 sprigs coriander

Method

Preheat the oven to 200°C/400°F/gas mark 6.

Remove the breasts from the quail. You can leave the wing bone on for decoration if you wish. If you do, scrape the bone clean. Season the quail well on both sides.

Heat the olive oil in a large frying pan and sear the quail breasts for 1 minute on each side, then transfer to the oven for 3 minutes. They will still be a little pink on the inside.

Finish cooking the risotto. Gently sauté the leek and carrot strips in the butter. Season well.

To serve

Add the chopped chives to the pumpkin risotto. Place a pastry cutter or ring on the centre of each plate and fill with risotto. Gently pat down the risotto and remove the rings.

Place some leek and carrot on the risotto and lay two quail breasts on top. Spoon some salsa around each plate and arrange a vanilla pod, some Parmesan shavings and three coriander/cilantro sprigs on each dish.

Mango and Coriander Salsa

Method

In a large bowl combine the stock syrup and the remaining ingredients. Keep the salsa refrigerated to retain its colour. The vanilla pod is used to infuse flavour and should be removed before serving.

1 recipe stock syrup (see page 151)
1 vanilla pod
1 mango, skinned and finely diced
50 g coriander, roughly chopped

[41]

Wine Suggestion

Two of the greatest wines with food, champagne and port, tend to be served before and after meals, rather than with them. Champagne is particularly versatile and works well with many starters. So if you are sipping an aperitif of champagne—or a good sparkling wine (Vouvray, for example)—you can keep drinking it with foie gras, smoked salmon or most salads. In the Champagne region, it is quite acceptable to drink bubbly throughout the meal. With a more complex starter such as this quail breast with risotto, a good rosé champagne will have plenty of pinot noir suppleness to balance the slight gaminess of these small birds; and at the same time the acidic lemony notes of chardonnay should work with the savoury fruitiness of pumpkin, coriander and mango. An alternative solution would be a good aromatic gewürztraminer from Alsace.

Crabmeat Salad with Lemon, Beetroot, Curried Crème Fraîche and Beetroot Chips

Fine and delicate crabmeat is very nicely balanced by sweet beetroot tossed with hazelnut oil and given added piquancy by curried crème fraîche.

Method

Flake the crabmeat into a bowl and discard any bone and filament. Mix with the cream, coriander and lemon zest. Season well and chill.

Scrape the carrots, but don't remove the green tops. Blanch in boiling salted water and refresh under cold running water. Cut the carrot into three pieces lengthwise and reserve for garnish.

Cook the beetroot in boiling salted water until just tender. It should be *al dente*. Drain and spread on a baking tray to cool, but don't rinse under cold water as the beetroot will lose some of its beautiful colour. Transfer to a small bowl.

Mix the champagne vinegar with the hazelnut oil and pour over the beetroot while still warm. Allow to cool fully and chill.

Mix the curry powder, crème fraîche and lemon juice gently. Don't overmix, or it will become too runny. Season well and chill.

To serve

Decorate each plate with small spoonfuls of beetroot. Place a ring or pastry cutter in the centre of each plate and spoon equal amounts of remaining beetroot into each base. Gently pat down and top with the crabmeat. Carefully remove the rings.

Using a piping bag with a 1 cm nozzle, pipe some curried crème fraîche on top of the crab. Dot the remaining crème fraîche around the plates. Dip 4 beetroot chips into the crème fraîche on top of the crab and place deep-fried julienne of beetroot and carrot on top.

Drizzle with some curry oil and beetroot oil. Garnish the plates with the baby carrots, citrus confit and coriander sprigs.

Serves 4

400 g cooked white crabmeat
100 ml cream
1 tablespoon fresh coriander leaves, roughly chopped
zest of 2 lemons
salt and freshly ground black pepper
8 baby carrots
120 g beetroot, peeled and diced
1 tablespoon champagne vinegar
2 tablespoons hazelnut oil
1 teaspoon curry powder
160 ml crème fraîche
juice of 2 lemons
16 beetroot chips (see page 126)
1 recipe deep-fried julienne of carrot (see page 128)
1 recipe deep-fried julienne of beetroot (see page 128)
2 tablespoons curry oil (see page 168)
1 tablespoon beetroot oil (see page 168)
1 recipe citrus confit (see page 142)
4 sprigs coriander

Crabmeat Salad with Lemon, Beetroot, Curried Crème Fraîche and Beetroot Chips

Wine Suggestion

A medium-dry chenin blanc from the Loire or South Africa is a good suggestion with crab. Vouvray is an excellent choice. But a young Muscadet-sur-lie, preferably from the excellent 1996 vintage, will also have the acidic structure and bouquet to deal with most seafood. There are complications in the form of the sweetness and spice of the curried crème fraîche, beetroot chips and citrus confit. For these, try a California fumé blanc, which will have the up-front acidity of sauvignon blanc without the aggressive grassiness of some other New World examples. Still another idea is a semillon/sauvignon blend from Bordeaux.

A Tart of Polenta with Marinated Plum Tomatoes, Goats' Cheese, Rocket Salad and Gazpacho Sauce

Warmed goats' cheese brings richness to polenta, with reduced balsamic vinegar to add flavour to rocket salad, garnished with a sauce of gazpacho

The polenta gives this pastry a crunchy texture that can stand up to the other ingredients. This is also a great supper or party dish—instead of making individual tarts, you could make a large tart and serve it with a tossed green salad. Another delicious filling is red onion, fennel and red pepper purée (see page 106).

Method
Preheat the oven to 190°C/375°F/gas mark 5.

Gently simmer the balsamic vinegar until reduced by half. Allow to cool and mix with the olive oil and basil leaves. Pour the mixture over the tomatoes and marinate for 3–4 minutes.

Place a round of goats' cheese in the base of each tart. Top with 2 tablespoons of tomato fondue and the drained tomato slices. Return to the oven for a further 5–10 minutes or until the tart is heated through—the cheese should be barely melting, not cooked. The tart is served warm, not hot.

To serve
Decorate the plates with cucumber and strips of roast pepper. Toss the rocket in the vinaigrette. Place a tart in the centre of each plate and pile some rocket on each tart. Spoon 2–3 tablespoons gazpacho sauce on to each plate, and garnish with the chives. Serve immediately.

Serves 4
1 recipe polenta pastry cases (see page 47)
50 ml balsamic vinegar
2 tablespoons olive oil
8 basil leaves, finely sliced
2 large plum tomatoes, thinly sliced
120 g goats' cheese, rinded and cut into 4 rounds
1 recipe tomato fondue (see page 49)

Garnishes
½ cucumber, cut into small balls with a parisienne cutter
1 red pepper, roasted and cut into strips (see page 128)
200 g rocket
1 recipe balsamic vinaigrette (see page 171)
1 recipe gazpacho sauce (see page 49)
1 small bunch of chives

Polenta Pastry Cases

In Peacock Alley, we use an even greater quantity of butter than in the recipe, but it then becomes very difficult to handle. Using the smaller quantity of butter, you should have no problems if the pastry is well chilled. However, even if a few cracks appear after baking blind, you can patch them with leftover bits of pastry, sealing the patches with a little beaten egg. The fillings for this pastry are all quite dry, so even if a crack remains, the fillings should stay in place.

Makes 4 small tarts
170 g plain flour
pinch of salt
70 g polenta
100 g unsalted butter
30 g Parmesan, finely grated
1 tablespoon basil, finely chopped
freshly ground black pepper
2 eggs
1 tablespoon olive oil

Method
Sift the flour and salt into a bowl, add the polenta and mix well. Rub in the butter until the mixture resembles breadcrumbs. Add the cheese and basil and season with pepper.

Beat the eggs with the olive oil and add to the flour mixture. Mix with your hands to form a firm pastry. Wrap the dough in clingfilm and chill for at least 30 minutes before use. This pastry can be kept in the fridge for up to 24 hours before using.

To bake blind
Preheat the oven to 190°C/375°F/gas mark 5.

Roll out the pastry to ½ cm thick. Line 4 tartlet tins or 1 x 30 cm flan ring with the pastry. Cover the pastry with greaseproof paper and fill the tart(s) with beans or rice. Bake for 10 minutes.

Remove the greaseproof paper and beans and return to the oven for a further 5 minutes to dry out. If the edges start to brown, place the tart on the bottom shelf or turn the oven down slightly. Make sure the pastry is well cooked and dry after you've baked it blind. This will ensure that the base will stay really crisp after the fillings have been added.

A Tart of Polenta with Marinated Plum Tomatoes, Goats' Cheese, Rocket Salad and Gazpacho Sauce

Tomato Fondue

Method
Heat the olive oil and sweat the shallots and garlic until soft, but do not allow to colour. Add the tomatoes, herbs and tomato purée. Gently simmer until all the liquid has evaporated and the mixture is quite dry. Season well and cool. Refrigerate until ready to use. It will keep overnight.

Serves 4

1 tablespoon olive oil
4 shallots, peeled and finely chopped
2 cloves garlic, peeled and crushed
8 plum tomatoes, skinned, deseeded and chopped
1 sprig thyme
1 sprig rosemary
1 tablespoon tomato purée
salt and freshly ground black pepper

Gazpacho Sauce

Gazpacho is a Spanish soup made with fresh tomatoes, red peppers, onions, cucumber, garlic and breadcrumbs. There are many variations, depending on where you are in Spain—it can be garnished with grapes and almonds, or made with a veal stock base, or sometimes served hot. We use our version of gazpacho as a dressing or sauce for our polenta tarts and also for garnishing some of our vegetarian dishes. If we want to serve it with a hot dish, we only warm it through, as it separates if overheated. You could also use it as an accompaniment to cold meats or fish.

Method
Place all the ingredients in a food processor and blend until smooth. Pass through a fine sieve and chill. Bring to room temperature and mix well before serving. The sauce can be made up to a day in advance.

Garnishes 4 tarts

2 shallots, peeled and roughly chopped
1 clove garlic, peeled and roughly chopped
6 tomatoes, skinned and deseeded
½ cucumber, peeled, deseeded and roughly chopped
1 chilli, deseeded and roughly chopped
½ teaspoon tomato purée
150 ml tomato juice
1 teaspoon sugar
1 teaspoon balsamic vinegar
salt and freshly ground black pepper

Wine Suggestion

A Loire Sancerre white, from the fine 1995 or 1996 vintages, will have the medium body and elegant fruitiness to balance the acidity of the tomatoes and gazpacho. A red Sancerre pinot noir, or other light reds from Bourgueil, will also work well with the goats' cheese. But the ideal combination for the crunchiness and texture of the polenta may be a northern Italian red, based on sangiovese, dolcetto or a young Barbera d'Asti (but beware the high tannins of some of the better Piedmontese reds).

Crab Spring Roll with Asian Greens and Hoi Sin Sauce

Soy sauce, wasabi, ginger and an optional garnish of whole chillies add up to a complex and spicy dish.

Method

Flake the crabmeat into a bowl and discard any bone and filament. Mix with the coriander, ginger, lemon zest and juice, cream and egg yolk. Season well. Shape into four sausage or spring roll shapes. Separate and spread out the ketaifi dough onto a clean work surface. Coat the crab with the ketaifi dough and chill for 1 hour.

Preheat the oven to 150°C/300°F/gas mark 2 and the deep fat fryer to 180°C. Heat the sesame oil in a medium-sized saucepan and sauté the bok choy and spring onions until starting to soften, Carefully deep fry the spring rolls for 1–2 minutes or until golden brown. Drain on kitchen paper and transfer to the oven. Add the shiitake mushrooms, peppers, soy sauce and chillies (optional) to the bok choy mixture. Sauté until soft.

To serve

Using a ring or pastry cutter to keep it in place, spoon the Asian green mixture onto each plate. Place a spring roll on top and then garnish the plates with some mango, wasabi crème fraîche, hoi sin sauce, lemon segments and coriander. Serve immediately.

Wine Suggestion

A full, herbaceous New Zealand sauvignon blanc should stand up to the spices. Another option is a New World blend of chardonnay and semillon with a fair amount of oak to add a degree of white chocolate sweetness. A full-bodied California chardonnay from the increasingly promising Sonoma County region should also do the job. A soft Australian or Chilean red could also cope with some of these flavours, but avoid anything too complex or tannic.

Serves 4

300 g cooked white crabmeat
2 tablespoons coriander, finely chopped
4 cm piece root ginger, peeled and very finely chopped
juice and zest of 1 lemon
30 ml cream
1 egg yolk
salt and freshly ground black pepper
150 g ketaifi dough (available in specialist shops)
vegetable oil for deep fat frying

Garnishes

2 tablespoons sesame oil
½ bok choy, shredded
½ bunch spring onions
75 g bean sprouts
4 shiitake mushrooms, finely sliced
2 roasted red peppers, sliced
1 tablespoon soy sauce
4 whole chillies (optional)
1 mango, finely diced
1 recipe wasabi crème fraîche
½ recipe hoi sin sauce (see page 72)
4 lemon segments (optional)
12–16 sprigs coriander

Crab Spring Roll with Asian Greens and Hoi Sin Sauce

Rocket Salad with Goats' Cheese Croûtons, Marinated Red Onions and Ginger and Basil Vinaigrette

Red onions marinaded in red wine and sugar add sweetness to rocket and red peppers

If you find it hard to buy rocket, you can use a selection of other lettuce leaves such as cos, frisée de Ruffée, oak leaf and curly endive and fresh herbs such as basil and coriander. Prepare the red onions at least a few hours ahead of time, as they need to cool in the red wine marinade before serving. Tomato bread is not essential for the croûtons—other breads are equally suitable.

Method

Heat the red wine and sugar in a small saucepan. Add the onion and simmer gently until soft, which should take about 5 minutes. Season with salt and pepper and allow to cool in the marinade for at least 2 hours. This can be made up to 24 hours in advance and the onions left in the marinade. They remain quite crisp.

Preheat the oven to 160°C/325°F/gas mark 3. Drain the onions and set aside. Cut the trimmed goats' cheese into four rounds. To make the croûtons, place one round of goats' cheese on each round of bread and bake for 5–10 minutes until heated through—the cheese should be barely melting—and set aside.

To serve

Decorate each plate with strips of pepper, tomatoes, chives and basil. Place a croûton in the centre of each plate. Toss the rocket with the ginger and basil dressing at the last minute and pile on top of the croûtons. Garnish with Parmesan shavings and serve immediately.

Serves 4

200 ml red wine
2 tablespoons sugar
2 red onions, peeled and thinly sliced
salt and freshly ground black pepper
100 g goats' cheese, rinded
4 rounds sundried tomato bread, approximately 2.5 cm thick (see page 163)
2 red peppers, roasted and cut into strips (see page 128)
2 tomatoes, skinned, seeded and chopped
small bunch of chives, chopped
4–8 basil leaves
200 g rocket or other lettuce and some fresh herbs
1 recipe ginger and basil vinaigrette (see page 170)

Garnish

Parmesan shavings

Wine Suggestion

Sauvignon blanc or viognier are again the grapes of choice here, but the red wine used for the marinated onions cries out for something to complement it. The gamay grape of Beaujolais, provided it is from a good vintage and a good Beaujolais Villages cru, has the youthful zest and low-tannin fruitiness to produce superb red wines for drinking with food. Try a 1995 or 1996 Fleurie, or for a little more darkness and depth, an older Morgon. And ignore the qualms of people who say Beaujolais is too light and lacking in structure to be anything other than a 'young' glugging drink. At its best, it is an excellent wine with many foods.

Pan-seared Turbot with Caramelised Onions, Overnight Baked Tomatoes, Goats' Cheese and Basil Mashed Potatoes

FISH

Pan-seared Turbot with Caramelised Onions, Overnight Baked Tomatoes, Goats' Cheese and Basil Mashed Potatoes

Rich ingredients in the mix, including the caramelised onions and the touch of Madeira, complement the succulent flavour and firm white flesh of one of the best sea fish.

This dish is quite simple to make, and the onion and goats' cheese garnish complements the turbot beautifully, without overpowering it. The potatoes are an essential part, to soak up all the delicious flavours of the fish and the bouillabaisse sauce. Be careful not to overcook the fish.

Method

Heat a tablespoon of olive oil in a medium-sized saucepan and sweat the red onions for 5 minutes without allowing them to colour. Add 50 g of butter and the sugar.

Turn up the heat slightly and after about 5 minutes the onions should turn golden brown and caramelise. Add the leeks and continue to sauté for a few minutes until the leeks have softened, then add the baked tomatoes and the spinach.

Remove from the heat and allow to cool for about 5 minutes. Fold in the goats' cheese (the cheese should not melt, which is why the mixture must cool slightly before it is added). Season with salt and pepper. Preheat the grill to its highest setting.

Heat the remaining olive oil in a frying pan. Season the turbot and place the fillets in the hot oil, skin side down, for about 1 minute, until the skin becomes crisp.

Turn the fillets over and add the remaining butter, Madeira, chicken stock, thyme and rosemary. Spoon the cooking liquor over the fish and transfer it to an ovenproof dish.

Finish cooking under the grill for 3–4 minutes, basting as often as possible with the cooking liquor. The fish is cooked when the flesh is barely firm to the touch. Discard the cooking liquor and herbs.

Gently reheat the bouillabaisse sauce, red onion mixture and basil mashed potatoes.

Serves 4

2 tablespoons olive oil
4 red onions, peeled and finely sliced
100 g butter
2 tablespoons sugar
4 leeks, finely chopped
1 recipe overnight baked tomatoes (see page 127)
200 g spinach, finely sliced
160 g goats' cheese, rind removed and roughly chopped
salt and freshly ground black pepper
4 x 150 g fillets of turbot, skin on
100 ml Madeira
100 ml chicken stock (see page 166)
2 sprigs thyme
2 sprigs rosemary
1 recipe basil mashed potatoes (see page 121)

Garnishes

1 recipe bouillabaisse sauce (see page 64)
4 deep-fried basil leaves (see page 128)

To serve

Place some of the red onion mixture in the centre of each plate. Spoon some of the bouillabaisse sauce around the plate and gently place the turbot fillets on top of the red onion mixture. Garnish with a deep-fried basil leaf. Place a quenelle of basil mashed potatoes on either side of the fish. Serve immediately.

Wine Suggestion

This needs a wine with some depth and a touch of judicious oakiness. A good bet is an older Montrachet or a Corton, in which the vanilla flavours from the oak will be balanced by the acidity of the finest white Burgundy. A Chilean or Australian chardonnay, provided they are not over-oaked, should also work well. For something a little more austere, try a dry Chablis to counterbalance some of the sweetness. Lighter red wines can also work well with richer fish dishes, for example a Chinon, Bourgueil or even a lighter pinot noir from a cool temperature region such as Oregon, or the light Spätburgunder style from Germany.

Pan-seared Salmon Fillet with Soft Herb Crust, Sauté Potatoes, Braised Chicory and Citrus Jus

Slightly smoky flavours of salmon seared at high temperatures blend well with chicory and a herb crust.

Method

Preheat the oven to 200°C/400°F/gas mark 6.

Run your fingers against the grain of the salmon to find the pin bones and remove them with tweezers. Mix the herbs together and spread them out on a chopping board.

Arrange the sauté potatoes on a baking tray with an onion ring and some baked tomato on each one. Bake for 10 minutes in the oven. At the same time reheat the braised chicory in the oven.

Heat the olive oil in a frying pan. Season the salmon with salt and pepper and sear the fillets on both sides, starting with the skin side down.

When the salmon is seared on both sides, remove from the pan and coat the skin side in the chopped herbs. Place in an ovenproof dish, herb side uppermost, and finish cooking in the oven for 5 minutes or until the flesh feels firm to the touch.

Reheat the citrus jus.

To serve

Place some chicory in the centre of each plate and arrange three sauté potatoes around it. Lay a salmon fillet on top of the chicory. Spoon some citrus jus around the plate. Garnish with dill oil, thyme and celeriac chips. Serve immediately.

Serves 4

4 x 150 g salmon fillets, skin on
1 tablespoon coriander, finely chopped
1 tablespoon chervil, finely chopped
1 tablespoon thyme, finely chopped
1 tablespoon tarragon, finely chopped
1 tablespoon lemon balm, finely chopped
1 recipe sauté potatoes (see page 60)
2 red onions, peeled and sliced into rings
½ recipe overnight baked tomatoes (see page 127)
1 recipe braised chicory (see page 60)
2 tablespoons olive oil
salt and freshly ground black pepper
200 ml citrus jus (see page 60)

Garnishes

100 ml dill oil (see page 168)
4 sprigs of thyme
1 recipe celeriac chips (see page 128)

Pan-seared Salmon Fillet with Soft Herb Crust, Sauté Potatoes, Braised Chicory and Citrus Jus

Braised Chicory

If you are making this in advance, add some lemon juice along with the chicken stock to prevent the chicory from discolouring. If you are serving it immediately you don't need the lemon juice.

Method
Preheat the oven to 200°C/400°F/gas mark 6.

Remove the outer leaves from the chicory and cut it into quarters lengthways. Heat the olive oil in a large frying pan, add the chicory and sprinkle with the sugar, salt and pepper. Cook until the sugar starts to caramelise.

Add the butter and continue to cook for another 3 minutes. Then slowly add the chicken stock and the lemon juice if using. Cook for another 2–3 minutes, then transfer to a roasting tin.

Roast for approximately 10 minutes until tender. Serve immediately, or allow to cool and reheat as necessary.

Serves 4

4 heads of chicory
2 tablespoons olive oil
1 tablespoon sugar
salt and freshly ground black pepper
50 g butter
100 ml chicken stock (see page 166)
2 tablespoons lemon juice (optional)

Sauté Potatoes

Method
Preheat the oven to 200°C/400°F/gas mark 6.

Cut the potatoes into slices 2 cm thick. Heat the butter in a frying pan and fry the potatoes on both sides until golden.

Add the stock, garlic and rosemary. Season to taste. Cook for a few minutes, allowing most of the stock to evaporate, and then transfer to a roasting tin and cook in the oven for about 10 minutes or until tender.

Serves 4

3 large potatoes, peeled
50 g butter
100 ml chicken or vegetable stock (see page 166/7)
1 clove garlic, peeled and thinly sliced
2 sprigs rosemary
salt and freshly ground black pepper

Citrus Jus

Heat the red wine vinegar in a medium-sized saucepan. Gently simmer until reduced by half and add the redcurrant jelly and red wine sauce. Continue to simmer until reduced by a third. Allow to cool fully and refrigerate until ready to use.

To serve
Reheat the sauce gently and add the zest and segments. Season with salt and pepper. Add the chives at the last minute and use as required.

Serves 4

50 ml red wine vinegar
2 tablespoons redcurrant jelly
1 recipe red wine sauce (see page 61)

Garnishes

zest and segments of 2 limes and 2 lemons
salt and freshly ground black pepper
1 small bunch of chives, finely chopped

Red Wine Sauce

This sauce is delicious served with beef and certain fish, but it overpowers lamb dishes. In Peacock Alley we start the sauce 24 hours ahead of time. The shallots, garlic and thyme are all marinated with the red wine for at least eight hours at room temperature. If you have the time and are organised enough to include this step, your sauce will have an even better flavour. Use a decent bottle of wine. The wine you cook with should be just as good as the wine you drink.

Serves 4

2 tablespoons olive oil
5 shallots, peeled and roughly chopped
3 cloves of garlic, peeled and roughly chopped
2 sprigs of thyme
salt and freshly ground black pepper
1 bottle of good red wine
2 tablespoons red wine vinegar
750 ml beef stock (see page 166)
30 g butter

Method

Heat the olive oil in a medium-sized saucepan, and sauté the shallots, garlic and thyme. Season lightly. Meanwhile place the red wine in a medium-sized saucepan and boil rapidly until reduced by two-thirds. Add the vinegar to the shallots and then slowly add about half the beef stock. Add the red wine reduction and the remaining stock. Reduce by half and season. Allow to cool and refrigerate until ready to use—the sauce will keep for 2–3 days. If using immediately, whisk in the butter and use as required.

Wine Suggestion

A New World chardonnay, or a chardonnay blend with semillon, will work. White Hermitage or white Chateauneuf-du-Pape will also work well. A grand cru Chablis will also have the finesse and power to match elements such as the braised chicory and baked tomatoes. But if others at your table want to have a red wine with meat or game dishes, do not be afraid to drink the red with your salmon—a fruity pinot noir, for example, or a light merlot from St Émilion or Chile. You could also try a Provence rosé.

Pan-seared Sea Bass with Fennel Purée, Fennel Confit, Spiced Lentils and Bouillabaisse Sauce

Delicate flavours of sea bass retain their subtlety alongside interesting flavours of lentils and bouillabaisse, with saffron aïoli as a garnish.

Method

Preheat the oven to 200°C/400°F/gas mark 6.

Run your fingers against the grain of the sea bass and remove any fine bones with tweezers. Wrap in clingfilm and refrigerate until ready to cook.

Using a sharp knife, remove the coarse stalks from the spinach leaves, but try to keep the leaves whole. Dip the leaves into boiling water for about 10 seconds, then remove and pat dry on kitchen paper or a clean tea towel. Place 4 rings or pastry cutters on a baking tray and line them with the spinach leaves.

Heat the spiced lentils in a small saucepan. Add the balsamic vinegar and cook over a medium heat until the mixture is quite dry. Add the roasted pepper, spring onions and chives, and mix well. Remove from the heat and use half the lentil mixture to line the base of each spinach parcel. Top with basil mashed potato and some fennel confit. Cut away any excess spinach hanging over the edge of the rings. Heat the parcels in the oven while you cook the fish.

Season the sea bass with salt and pepper. Heat the olive oil in a large frying pan and cook the fillets, skin side down, for 1½ minutes. Turn the fish over and add the butter, rosemary, Madeira and chicken stock. Baste with the cooking liquor and finish cooking in the oven for 3–5 minutes or until the flesh is firm to the touch.

In separate saucepans, reheat the remaining lentil mixture, the bouillabaisse sauce and the fennel purée.

To serve

Spoon some fennel purée around the centre of each plate. Leave a small gap and spoon some bouillabaisse sauce around the purée. Place a spinach parcel on the centre of each plate and gently remove the rings. Top with the sea bass and garnish with the chive oil, tomato oil, a tablespoon of lentils, aïoli and chervil. Serve immediately.

Serves 4

4 x 120 g fillets of sea bass, skin on
12 large spinach leaves
200 g spiced lentils (see page 116)
1 tablespoon balsamic vinegar
½ roasted red pepper, cut into strips (see page 128)
2 spring onions, finely chopped
1 small bunch chives, finely chopped
100 g basil mashed potatoes (see page 121)
1 recipe confit of fennel (see page 123)
salt and freshly ground black pepper
1 tablespoon olive oil
50 g butter
4 sprigs rosemary
2 tablespoons Madeira
60 ml chicken stock (see page 166)
200 ml bouillabaisse sauce (see page 64)
100 ml fennel purée (see page 64)

Garnishes

60 ml chive oil (see page 169)
60 ml tomato oil (see page 169)
40 ml saffron aïoli (see page 68)
12 sprigs of chervil

Pan-seared Sea Bass with Fennel Purée, Fennel Confit, Spiced Lentils and Bouillabaisse Sauce

Fennel Purée

This goes very well with most fish and chicken dishes.

Method
Remove the feathery green tops and the roots from the fennel bulbs and discard. Roughly chop the bulbs.

Heat the olive oil in a medium-sized saucepan and sauté the chopped fennel for 3 minutes, but do not allow it to colour.

Add the lemon juice, butter, salt and pepper. Continue to sauté for another minute and then add the chicken stock. Cook gently for a further 20 minutes.

Remove from the heat and blend in a food processor. Pass the mixture through a fine sieve, using the back of a small ladle to help push it through. Check the seasoning and reheat as necessary.

Serves 4
2 fennel bulbs
50 ml olive oil
juice of 1 lemon
30 g butter
salt and freshly ground black pepper
125 ml chicken stock (see page 166)

Bouillabaisse Sauce

Don't worry if you can't get any prawn shells—the sauce will still taste wonderful. Remember to keep the lid of your saucepan handy to cover the flame if it gets too high.

Method
Heat the olive oil in a medium-sized saucepan, and sauté the fennel trimmings, shallots, garlic, herbs and spices until the fennel and shallots are soft. Season with salt and pepper and add the prawn shells.

Pour the cognac and Pernod into a ladle. Heat the ladle over a flame, then gently tip it forward so that the alcohol lights. Pour this into the saucepan immediately and allow the flame to go out.

Add the plum tomatoes and the tomato purée. Slowly add the chicken stock and bring to the boil, then reduce the heat and simmer for 30 minutes, skimming any fat or impurities from the surface, using a metal spoon.

Remove from the heat and pass through a sieve into a clean saucepan. Reduce to taste, by as much as half. Adjust the seasoning and reheat as necessary.

Serves 4
2 tablespoons olive oil
20 g fennel trimmings (feathery tips and root)
6 shallots, peeled and chopped
4 cloves of garlic, peeled and chopped
2 sprigs of rosemary
2 sprigs of thyme
pinch of saffron
pinch of cayenne
salt and freshly ground black pepper
50 g prawn shells (optional)
30 ml cognac
30 ml Pernod
4 plum tomatoes, halved and deseeded
2 tablespoons tomato purée
600 ml chicken stock (see page 166)

Wine Suggestion

The fish in itself calls for a well-balanced mature white wine, from Burgundy or Alsace. But the spiced lentils, fennel and aïoli call for something more assertive—a full-bodied, cool-temperature fermentation Graves from Pessac-Léognan, or a herbaceous sauvignon blanc from New Zealand. A dry riesling or chenin blanc will also stand up well to the spices.

Pan-seared Monkfish with Pumpkin Purée, Sauté Cabbage, Roasted Salsify, Sundried Tomato Tapenade and Saffron Aïoli

The firm flesh and sturdy flavour of monkfish allow for robust treatment and rich flavouring.

Method

Preheat the oven to 150°C/300°F/gas mark 2.

Heat two tablespoons of olive oil in a large frying pan and sauté the salsify and shallots. Allow them to take on some colour and then add the sugar and 25 g of the butter. Season with salt and pepper and transfer to an ovenproof dish when the vegetables start to caramelise. Add two tablespoons of chicken stock, cover with tinfoil and bake for 25–30 minutes or until tender. Turn the oven up to 200°C/400°F/gas mark 6.

Heat a tablespoon of olive oil and 25 g of the butter in a medium-sized saucepan and sauté the cabbage until just starting to wilt, then add the leek and half the spring onions. Add the spinach and season well. Set aside.

In a large saucepan combine the roasted salsify and shallots with the spiced lentils and red pepper. Gently heat through.

Reheat the pumpkin purée with a little butter and chicken stock. Reheat the cabbage mixture.

Heat the remaining olive oil in a large frying pan. Season the monkfish with salt and pepper and then quickly sear it on all sides. Add the rosemary, Madeira and the remaining butter and chicken stock. Baste the fish with the cooking liquor and transfer it to an ovenproof dish. Finish cooking in the oven for 5 minutes or until the flesh is firm to the touch.

To serve

Place some tapenade, aïoli and beurre blanc on each plate. Place some of the cabbage mixture in the centre of each plate and top with the pumpkin purée. Arrange some of the spiced lentil mixture around and place a monkfish fillet on top of the purée. Garnish with sprigs of chervil and chives and deep-fried spinach. Serve immediately.

Serves 4

4 tablespoons olive oil
12 salsify, peeled
12 shallots, peeled
2 teaspoons sugar
100 g butter
salt and freshly ground black pepper
60 ml chicken stock (see page 166)
¼ Savoy cabbage, shredded
½ leek, finely chopped
2 spring onions, finely chopped
40 g spinach, finely sliced
100 g spiced lentils (see page 116)
1 roasted red pepper, cut into strips (see page 128)
1 recipe pumpkin purée (see page 115)
4 x 120 g monkfish fillets
4 sprigs rosemary
60 ml Madeira
40 g sundried tomato tapenade (see page 69)
40 ml saffron aïoli (see page 68)
80 ml lemon and lime beurre blanc (see page 68)

Garnishes

12 sprigs chervil
1 small bunch chives, chopped
1 recipe deep-fried spinach (see page 128)

Pan-seared Monkfish with Pumpkin Purée, Sauté Cabbage, Roasted Salsify, Sundried Tomato Tapenade and Saffron Aïoli

Lemon and Lime Beurre Blanc

Technically speaking, this is not a true beurre blanc due to the addition of cream. However, the cream makes it more stable and stops the sauce from separating as quickly. Beurre blanc originated in the Loire valley, in the Nantes and Anjou regions, where it was made from Muscadet wine and local butter. Apparently, a chef was trying to make a béarnaise sauce but forgot about the eggs! Thus the beurre blanc was born.

Method

Heat the oil in a small saucepan and sweat the shallots with the rosemary and thyme. When the shallots are soft and transparent, add the lemon and lime zest and juice and the wine. Increase the heat and reduce by half.

Add the cream and reduce again by half. Remove from the heat and whisk in the butter gradually.

Pass through a fine sieve and season with salt and pepper. The sauce should be made as close to serving as possible, but can be kept warm in a bain marie for about 15 minutes. Make sure the water is kept hot, not boiling. Keep checking the water level, topping up when necessary.

Serves 4

1 tablespoon olive oil
4 shallots, peeled and very finely chopped
1 sprig rosemary
1 sprig thyme
zest and juice of 1 lemon
zest and juice of 1 lime
2 tablespoons white wine
75 ml cream
200 g unsalted butter, diced and well chilled
salt and freshly ground white pepper

Saffron Aïoli

Heat a tablespoon of olive oil with the saffron strands. Remove from the heat and add the sunflower oil and remaining olive oil. Allow to infuse for up to an hour.

Place the egg yolks, garlic, mustard, salt and pepper in a food processor and blend until smooth. Leave the food processor on and slowly pour the oils into the mixture. Allow the mixture to thicken after each addition of oil before adding more. Gradually incorporate the white wine vinegar and lemon juice into the aïoli. Check the seasoning and chill. Use within 12 hours.

Serves 4

2 tablespoons olive oil
1 pinch of saffron strands
120 ml sunflower oil
2 egg yolks
1 clove of garlic, peeled and crushed
1 teaspoon Dijon mustard
salt and freshly ground white pepper
1 tablespoon white wine vinegar
juice of 1 lemon

Sundried Tomato Tapenade

Blend all the ingredients together in a food processor until very fine in texture. Pass through a fine sieve, using the back of a ladle to help push it through. Readjust seasoning if necessary and serve. The tapenade will keep for a week if stored in the fridge in a glass jar, topped with olive oil and sealed.

Wine Suggestion

Rich and complex garnishes make this a dish demanding either a very austere white—a crisp Chablis, which could lose some of its own delicacy to the dish—or a richer New World chardonnay. Big Australian oaky styles may work, but beware the overwhelming vanilla flavours of overt oaking. A better choice might be a Sonoma County reserve from California—a little cooler in style, but still full-bodied enough to balance the muscularity of monkfish. Red Burgundy could also be good with this dish—a Volnay, for example, or even a Gevrey-Chambertin with depth and complex flavours. You could also try a lighter style of Côtes du Rhône Villages—a young Vacqueyras, for example.

Serves 4

125 g sundried tomatoes in oil, drained
125 g black olives, stoned
1 small bunch chives, roughly chopped
1 tablespoon parsley
2 cloves garlic, peeled and roughly chopped
1 tablespoon anchovy paste
salt and freshly ground black pepper
50 ml olive oil

Tournedos of Tuna with Sesame Crust, Asian Greens and Hoi Sin Sauce

The combinations of flavours in this dish are superb. Tuna is best served medium-rare or medium, as it tends to dry out if you cook it to the 'well done' stage and starts to resemble what you find in tins. Initially some customers in Peacock Alley are hesitant about eating fish this rare, but once they have tasted it, they are immediately converted.

Marinating the tuna in a strong Asian marinade, although not strictly necessary, makes a big difference to the flavour. If you cannot find tuna, you could use swordfish instead.

Method

Mix together 50 ml sesame oil, the olive oil, 50 ml hoi sin sauce, garlic, salt and pepper and marinate the tuna steaks for about an hour.

Mix the wasabi with a small amount of crème fraîche, then gradually add the remaining crème fraîche, and mix well. Refrigerate until ready to use.

Preheat the oven to 200°C/400°F/gas mark 6.

Heat the remaining sesame oil (2 tablespoons) in a large saucepan, and sauté the bok choy and spring onions until starting to soften. Remove from the heat. Blanch the okra and samphire in boiling salted water for 30 seconds. Refresh under cold water and place in a small saucepan with the butter.

When you are ready to cook the tuna, start reheating the bok choy mixture, and add the beansprouts, mushrooms, roasted peppers and soy sauce. Gently heat the okra and samphire in the butter. Season. Heat the remaining hoi sin sauce. In a large frying pan, heat two tablespoons of the tuna marinade. Season the tuna fillets, and when the pan is smoking sear the tuna quickly on both sides. Remove from the pan and dip one side of each tuna fillet in the beaten egg, and then in the sesame seeds. Transfer to the oven for 2–3 minutes.

To serve

While the tuna is in the oven, garnish the plates with the bok choy mixture, okra and samphire, 1–2 tablespoons of hoi sin sauce, dried chillies, curry oil, coriander and small amounts of wasabi crème fraîche. Place a tuna fillet on each plate and serve immediately.

Serves 4

80 ml sesame oil
100 ml olive oil
1 recipe hoi sin sauce (see page 72)
2 cloves garlic, peeled and crushed
salt and freshly ground black pepper
½ teaspoon wasabi
80 g crème fraîche
4 tuna fillets, each weighing 200 g
1 bok choy, shredded
1 bunch spring onions, finely chopped
16 okra, heads removed
50 g samphire
20 g butter
100 g beansprouts
4 shiitake mushrooms, finely sliced
2 roasted red peppers, sliced
2 tablespoons soy sauce
1 egg, beaten
50 g sesame seeds, toasted

Garnishes

3 dried chillies, finely chopped
100 ml curry oil (see page 168)
12–16 sprigs coriander

Tournedos of Tuna with Sesame Crust, Asian Greens and Hoi Sin Sauce

Hoi Sin Sauce

This is a good sauce for Chinese/Japanese-style food or for marinating and basting chicken or meat on the barbecue. You could also make an Asian salad dressing from this sauce by whisking in sesame oil to taste. For a delicious supper dish marinate some chicken breasts in the hoi sin sauce and pan fry. Dip the chicken in sesame seeds and finish cooking in the oven.

Method

Sweat together the olive oil, shallots, garlic and ginger until the shallots are soft.

Add the lemon grass and then slowly add the red wine sauce or stock. Bring to the boil and add the soy sauce, hoi sin sauce and honey. Taste and reduce if necessary until you achieve the desired taste. The sauce will keep for a few days in the fridge.

Wine Suggestion

Rare tuna can be drunk with light reds, but the overall balance of flavours in this dish suggests a white wine with plenty of acidity and body (Champagne could do the job quite well). Soy and hoi sin sauce will go best with a New World sauvignon blanc, or a medium-dry riesling. Something different to try is Bourgogne aligoté. The aligoté grape, in good years, has a tart, lemony bouquet and a good deal of aromatic fruitiness. Gewürztraminer would be a more orthodox choice for its spiciness, but it can be highly aromatic and too dominant for some food.

Serves 4

1 tablespoon olive oil

4 shallots, peeled and roughly chopped

3 cloves garlic, peeled and roughly chopped

2 cm piece root ginger, peeled and sliced

2 stalks lemon grass, roughly chopped

200 ml red wine sauce (see page 61) or chicken or vegetable stock (see page 166/7)

100 ml soy sauce

75 ml hoi sin sauce (available in Asian food stores)

2–3 tablespoons honey

Pan-seared Salmon with a Skin of Couscous, Fondue of Leek and Tomato, Buttered Jumbo Asparagus, and Sauce Vert

The couscous crust works really well with the salmon, but wouldn't necessarily suit all fish—perhaps this is because salmon is quite fatty. This dish is full of beautiful spring and summer colours.

Method

Preheat the oven to 200°C/400°F/gas mark 6.

Run your fingers against the grain of the salmon to find the pin bones and remove them with tweezers. When you are ready to cook the salmon, gently reheat the garnishes.

Season the salmon with salt and pepper.

Heat the olive oil in a large frying pan. Spread the couscous on a clean work surface or large plate. Dip the largest side of the salmon into the beaten egg and then into the couscous.

Sear the salmon, couscous side down first, in the hot olive oil and then sear the remaining three sides. Be careful not to damage the couscous crust. Transfer to the oven and finish cooking for 5 minutes.

Place a ring or pastry cutter in the centre of each plate and fill with equal amounts of the fondue of leek and tomato. Arrange the asparagus in a criss-cross pattern outside the rings, and spoon some of the sauce vert around the plates. Remove the rings and gently place the salmon fillets on top of the fondue with the couscous side uppermost. Serve immediately.

Serves 4

4 x 120 g thick salmon fillets, skinned
salt and freshly ground black pepper
3 tablespoons olive oil
100 g couscous
1 egg, beaten

Garnishes

1 recipe buttered jumbo asparagus (see page 75)
1 recipe fondue of leek and tomato (see below)
1 recipe sauce vert (see page 75)

Fondue of Leek and Tomato

Method

Heat the olive oil in a medium-sized saucepan and sweat the leeks for 5 minutes until soft. Add the butter, cook for another minute and season lightly. At this stage you could set the mixture aside until you are ready to complete the recipe. Add the tomatoes and cook over a higher heat until any excess liquid evaporates. Add the chives and serve.

Serves 4

2 tablespoons olive oil
6 leeks, finely sliced
30 g butter
salt and freshly ground black pepper
½ recipe overnight baked tomatoes (see page 127), roughly chopped
1 small bunch chives, finely chopped

At Peacock Alley we make all our own bread.

Buttered Jumbo Asparagus

Different varieties of asparagus range from white to purple to green. The white variety tends to be very tender, but has little flavour when compared to the green varieties, which are considered superior.

Method

Using a vegetable peeler, peel the asparagus, starting just below the tip. Cut away the coarse ends of the stalks but reserve these for the sauce vert. Cut the remaining asparagus in half.

Blanch or steam the stalkier halves for 2–3 minutes, add the remainder (the tip halves) and cook for a further 2–3 minutes. Refresh under cold running water and set aside until ready to serve. Heat the butter in a large frying pan, add the almonds and asparagus, and cook over a high heat for 2–3 minutes. Season lightly and serve.

Serves 4
800 g jumbo asparagus
75 g butter
30 g almonds, peeled and sliced
salt and freshly ground black pepper

Sauce Vert

Technically speaking, a sauce vert is a green mayonnaise. The Peacock Alley version is a rich, creamy, bright green sauce, perfect with fish.

Method

Cook the asparagus in boiling salted water until tender. Drain and set aside. Heat the butter in a medium-sized saucepan and sauté the spinach until just starting to wilt.

Transfer to a food processor/blender along with the asparagus and stock. Process until smooth. Season well and gently heat in a medium-sized saucepan. Bring the cream to the boil and gradually whisk it into the purée. Strain and reheat as necessary.

100 g asparagus trimmings
50 g butter
200 g spinach
400 ml vegetable or chicken stock
  (see page 166/7)
salt and freshly ground black pepper
200 ml cream

Wine Suggestion

Asparagus are always difficult to match with wine, but sauvignon blanc is perhaps the professional choice. The addition of butter suggests a light, unoaked chardonnay, or a New World blend of sauvignon and chardonnay. The salmon itself has plenty of natural oiliness and can easily take a light red, perhaps a Loire cabernet franc.

Crabcake with Basil Pesto Couscous, Ratatouille and Gazpacho Sauce

Deep-fried crabcake with coriander, lemon juice and egg yolks contrasts with North African notes of couscous, ketaifi and gazpacho.

All the colours and flavours of the Mediterranean are combined in this dish, which is relatively easy to prepare. Everything except the crabcake can be made a few hours in advance and reheated. The crabcakes can be made an hour in advance, and left to chill. They take only a few minutes to cook.

Method

Flake the crabmeat into a bowl and discard any bone and filament. Mix with the coriander, parsley, lemon zest, juice, cream and egg yolks. Season well. Shape into four balls. Separate and spread out the ketaifi dough on a clean work surface. Coat the crab mixture with the dough and chill for an hour before deep frying.

Preheat the oven to 150°C/300°F/gas mark 2 and the deep fat fryer to 180°C. Gently reheat the garnishes. Carefully deep-fry the crabcakes for about 2 minutes or until golden brown. Drain on kitchen paper and transfer to the oven while you garnish the plates.

To serve

Using a ring or pastry cutter to keep its shape, spoon equal amounts of couscous on to the centre of each plate. Top with ratatouille and carefully remove the ring. Place a crabcake on top and spoon some gazpacho sauce around the plate. Serve immediately.

Note: For the couscous and ratatouille tower to hold its shape the consistency has to be perfect. If you are worried it will collapse, simply spoon some couscous and ratatouille on to each plate, place a crabcake on the side and drizzle the plate with gazpacho sauce.

Wine Suggestion

A dish redolent of Keats' 'beaker full of the warm south' would appreciate a warm weather Mediterranean wine, perhaps the cabernet sauvignon-based Château Musar from Lebanon. A Greek white from the volcanic isles of Crete or Santorini, or a resiny Retsina, will also work.

Serves 4
500 g cooked white crabmeat
2 tablespoons coriander, finely chopped
1 tablespoon parsley, finely chopped
zest and juice of 2 lemons
50 ml cream
2 egg yolks
salt and freshly ground black pepper
300 g ketaifi dough (available in specialist shops)
vegetable oil for deep fat frying

Garnishes
1 recipe pesto couscous (see page 115)
1 recipe ratatouille (see page 123)
1 recipe gazpacho sauce (see page 49)

Roasted Scallops with Fennel Cream and Capellini Cakes

Good scallops are among the very best seafood, particularly picked by hand by scuba divers. Seared fast and served immediately, they go well with the delicately flavoured fennel cream

It is important to remove the coral and the small moon-shaped muscle from the white meat, which become very tough when cooked. In Europe, though not in North America, the coral is used to flavour sauces. In Peacock Alley we always pay extra for dived scallops, as the dredged ones can retain a lot of sand. Raw scallops should have a sweet smell, which indicates freshness.

Serves 4
1 recipe capellini cakes (see page 78)
½ recipe overnight baked tomatoes (see page 127)
1 recipe fennel cream (see below)
50 ml olive oil
12–16 scallops
salt and freshly ground black pepper
100 g butter
1 sprig of rosemary
20 g rocket

Method

Preheat the oven to 150°C/300°F/gas mark 2. Reheat the capellini cakes and overnight baked tomatoes in the oven. Gently reheat the fennel cream.

Heat the olive oil in a large frying pan. Season the scallops with salt and pepper, and sear on both sides until golden. Add the butter and rosemary. Baste the scallops with the melted butter and then remove from the heat.

To serve

Place a capellini cake topped with overnight baked tomatoes on each plate and garnish with rocket leaves. Carefully place 3–4 scallops on top, drizzle the plates with some fennel cream and serve immediately.

Fennel Cream

Method

Remove the feathery green tops and roots from the fennel bulb and discard. Roughly chop the fennel.

Heat the olive oil in a medium-sized saucepan and sauté the chopped fennel for three minutes, but do not allow it to colour. Add the lemon juice, butter, salt and pepper. Continue to sauté for another minute and then add the chicken stock. Cook gently for 15 minutes. Add the cream and cook for a further 5 minutes.

Remove from the heat and blend in a food processor until smooth. Pass through a fine sieve using the back of a ladle to help push it through. Check the seasoning and reheat as necessary.

Garnishes 4
1 fennel bulb
2 tablespoons olive oil
juice of ½ lemon
20 g butter
salt and freshly ground black pepper
60 ml chicken stock
60 ml cream

Capellini Cakes

These little pasta cakes are similar to potato röstis, but are quicker and easier to make. They also make good accompaniments to game dishes.

Method
Cook the pasta in plenty of boiling water with a tablespoon of olive oil for 2–3 minutes or until *al dente*. Drain and toss with 50 ml olive oil, the butter and parmesan and season well.

Divide the pasta into four 8 cm rings. Heat a tablespoon of olive oil in a large frying pan. Place a fish slice under the rings and transfer them to the frying pan. Fry the pasta for 1–2 minutes on each side, using the ring to keep the shape.

Serve the cakes immediately or allow them to cool. When ready to serve reheat the cakes in the oven at 150°C/300°F/gas mark 2 for about 5 minutes.

Wine Suggestion

If the scallops are the large, cold-water specimens, it would be a pity to overpower them with robust wines. Good white Burgundy such as Meursault would be ideal, as would a fine New Zealand chardonnay such as Cloudy Bay, or a decent sparkling wine. Most good Loire whites, including Muscadet sur lie, should also be fine. Some lighter styles of red wine may also work, but avoid oaky New World styles—the vanilla flavours imparted by oak barrels tend to be cloying with delicate seafood dishes.

Serves 4
200 g capellini
2 tablespoons olive oil
50 ml olive oil
50 g butter
2 tablespoons parmesan, finely grated
salt and freshly ground black pepper

Fillet of Beef with Roast Shallots, Shallot Purée, Spaghetti of Vegetables and Parmesan Tuiles

MEAT, GAME
AND POULTRY

Fillet of Beef with Roast Shallots, Shallot Purée, Spaghetti of Vegetables and Parmesan Tuiles

Fillets are an important aspect of meat dishes in classical cooking, but here a modern treatment adds a lighter touch with roast shallots and a beef jus.

Fillets are without doubt the best cut of beef, well known for their exquisite tenderness and their association with luxurious accompaniments such as foie gras and truffles. They also go beautifully with potato röstis, shallots, wild mushrooms, and beef sauces made with red wine.

Method

Wrap the fillets tightly in cling film, and leave to rest overnight if possible. This will help keep them in a neat shape. Prepare all the garnishes you would like to use well in advance, so that they only need reheating. Preheat oven to 200°C/400°F.

Remove the cling film from the fillets and season generously. Reheat the garnishes. Heat the olive oil in a large frying pan and when the pan is smoking sear the fillets on both sides and then transfer to the oven to finish cooking for 5–10 minutes depending on how rare you like it.

To serve

Place a fillet in the centre of each plate and top with spaghetti of vegetables and a Parmesan tuile. Spoon some shallot purée around the fillet and some beef jus and roast shallots around the purée. Garnish with sprigs of coriander and serve immediately.

Shallot Purée

Method

Sweat the shallots and garlic in the olive oil and butter until the shallots become transparent. Do not allow them to take on any colour. Add the chicken stock, bring to the boil, boil rapidly until reduced by half. Take off the heat and cool slightly before processing in a blender or food processor until smooth. Pass through a fine sieve. Adjust the seasoning and reheat as necessary.

Serves 4

4 beef fillets, each weighing about 200 g
salt and freshly ground black pepper
1 tablespoon olive oil
1 recipe roast shallots (see page 90)
1 recipe shallot purée (see below)
1 recipe beef jus (see page 82)
1 recipe spaghetti of vegetables (see page 82)
4 Parmesan tuiles (see page 82)
12 sprigs coriander

Serves 4

8 shallots, peeled and roughly chopped
1 clove garlic, peeled and roughly chopped
1 tablespoon olive oil
30 g butter
300 ml chicken stock (see page 166)
salt and freshly ground black pepper

Beef Jus

Method

Reduce the beef stock by one-third and then whisk in the butter and olive oil. Adjust the seasoning and serve.

Serves 4
750 ml beef stock (see page 166)
75 g butter
2 tablespoons olive oil

Spaghetti of Vegetables

Gently sauté the leeks and carrots in the butter. Season and use as required.

Garnishes 4
2 leeks, finely sliced into long julienne strips
2 carrots, peeled and finely sliced
50 g butter
salt and freshly ground black pepper

Parmesan Tuiles

Method

Mix all the ingredients together. Have ready a roasting tin filled with cold water. Place a small nonstick frying pan over a high heat. Place a 4–6 cm ring in the centre of the pan and sprinkle a quarter of the Parmesan mixture into the ring. Remove the ring and cook the Parmesan mixture over a high heat until the edges start to turn brown.

Dip the base of the pan into the cold water to set the tuile. Remove the tuile and place on a wire rack and start the process again to make the other three tuiles. Make the tuiles a few hours in advance and cool. Reheat in a warm oven before serving.

Yields 4 tuiles
100 g freshly grated Parmesan
25 g chopped herbs—parsley, coriander or chervil
1 tablespoon flour
salt and freshly ground black pepper

Wine Suggestion

Good Bordeaux is an excellent choice with a fillet. All the top Bordeaux wines, from Latour to Le Pin, depend upon 'big' tannins for their structure and ageing potential; and a fillet—preferably rare—will soften and complement the harder tannins which stop the greatest wines from ageing prematurely. But picking a wine to go with a tender cut of beef is very much a matter of individual taste—a Léoville-Barton from St Julien, perhaps, with rare fillet, or a softer St Émilion grand cru with fillet served medium or well-done.

Suprême of Chicken with Spinach and Parmesan, Basil Pesto Barley Risotto and Harissa

Chicken stuffed with leek, spinach, rocket and chives complements grilled aubergines and barley risotto.

Sundried Tomato Tapenade (see page 69) and Chilli Polenta (see page 117) also go really well with this dish. The garnishes listed below aren't strictly necessary for home cooking.

Method

Preheat the oven to 200°C/400°F/gas mark 6.

Start with the stuffing. Heat half the butter and 1 tablespoon of olive oil in a large saucepan, and gently cook the garlic for approximately 2 minutes. Add the leek and cook for a further 2 minutes, then add the spinach, rocket, chives and lettuce. Mix well and cool before adding the Parmesan and egg yolk. Season well and cool fully.

Heat 1 tablespoon of olive oil and fry the aubergine and onion on all sides. Season well and transfer to a baking tray. Finish cooking in the oven for 10–15 minutes. Drizzle the aubergines with more olive oil if they start to dry out. Make a horizontal slit in each chicken suprême and season well. Insert some stuffing into each slit but do not overstuff—the stuffing should not spill out of the incision.

Heat the remaining butter and 1 tablespoon of olive oil in a large frying pan. Cook the chicken over a high heat, skin side down, for approximately 3–4 minutes. Transfer to the oven and continue cooking for 7–10 minutes.

To serve

Heat the risotto. Arrange some harissa around each plate and pile some risotto in the centre of each dish. Place a grilled aubergine slice on top of the risotto and lay a chicken suprême on top. Place a tablespoon of aubergine purée on top of the chicken. Stick some aubergine chips into the harissa and the purée. Arrange some garlic confit around the harissa. Spoon about 1 tablespoon each of dill oil and tomato oil around the dish. Garnish with sprigs of thyme, flat leaf parsley and lemon confit.

Serves 4

60 g butter
3 tablespoons olive oil
2 cloves garlic, peeled and crushed
½ leek (white part only), finely chopped
100 g spinach, stalks removed
100 g rocket
1 small bunch chives, chopped
¼ head frisée lettuce, roughly chopped
80 g Parmesan, grated
1 egg yolk
salt and freshly ground black pepper
½ aubergine, sliced into 4 equal rounds
1 red onion, peeled and quartered
4 suprêmes of chicken, skin on
1 recipe basil pesto barley risotto (see page 114–5)
1 recipe harissa (see page 85)

Garnishes

½ recipe aubergine purée (see page 94)
1 recipe aubergine chips (see page 125)
1 recipe confit of garlic (see page 124)
40 ml dill oil (see page 168)
60 ml tomato oil (see page 169)
4 sprigs of thyme
12 sprigs of flat leaf parsley
1 recipe citrus confit (see page 142)

Suprême of Chicken with Spinach and Parmesan, Basil Pesto Barley Risotto and Harissa

Harissa

Harissa, which is similar to chilli jam, originated in north Africa. It can be used to accompany meat, and is delicious with couscous which, unless very well seasoned, can be bland. The addition of sugar reduces the strength of the chillies.

Method

Soak the chillies in water for an hour, using just enough water to cover. Remove them from the water and dry very well. Reserve some of this 'chilli water'. Using a food processor, blend the chillies and all the other ingredients, except the oil, with a tablespoon of the chilli water to make a chunky paste.

Add the oil slowly until you have a thick jam-like consistency. Try not to overprocess, as the harissa looks nicer with a little texture. Check the seasoning and keep covered in the fridge until ready to use. Harissa can be kept for up to a week.

Wine Suggestion

This is a rich, user-friendly dish calling for a big, layered red from southern France, Italy or Spain. Some superb examples are coming out of Bandol in Provence, from Gigondas and Cornas in the Rhône, and in tempranillo varietals from Spain. A good Brunello from Italy should do well. Blends of grenache, with mourvèdre, for example, will also work. Among whites, New World chardonnay from Chile or South Africa should be fine.

Yields 100 g
75 g dried red chillies, chopped
2 cloves garlic, peeled
1 tablespoon coriander leaves
¼ teaspoon caraway seeds, ground
1 teaspoon cumin, roasted and ground
sea salt
1 tablespoon tomato purée
1 tablespoon sugar
50 ml olive oil

Daube with Roast Shallots, Morel Cream, Braised Carrots and Rosemary Mashed Potatoes

Daube with Roast Shallots, Morel Cream, Braised Carrots and Rosemary Mashed Potatoes

The daube was traditionally a cooking vessel, ideal for intense meat stews such as these ox cheeks make.

Method

Trim the ox cheeks really well, removing as much fat as you can. If you have time marinate them in the red wine overnight with a little salt and freshly ground black pepper.

Preheat the oven to 200°C/400°F/gas mark 6. Pat the ox cheeks dry and season with plenty of salt and pepper. Heat the olive oil in a frying pan and sear the ox cheeks on all sides. Transfer to a large ovenproof dish. Return the frying pan to the heat and deglaze with about 100 ml red wine. Add the shallots and simmer for 2–3 minutes. Transfer to a large saucepan and add the rest of the red wine along with the garlic, rosemary, thyme and chicken stock. Heat thoroughly.

Pour this mixture over the ox cheeks and cook in the oven for 3°–4 hours, or until the meat is cooked through and extremely tender. Turn the ox cheeks every ½ hour and baste with the cooking liquor. About 15 minutes before the ox cheeks are cooked, make the morel mushroom cream. Heat the butter in a medium-sized saucepan. Finely chop a third of the morels and sauté in the butter. Add the cream and reduce by half. Make the hollandaise sauce and keep it warm in a bain marie. Remove the ox cheeks from the cooking liquor and return them to the oven to dry out for 5–10 minutes. Reheat the potato, spinach, carrots and tomatoes.

Add 3–5 tablespoons of the cooking liquor, the remaining whole morels and the roast shallots to the morel cream. Reheat, season well and add the chopped chives at the last minute. Remove the ox cheeks from the oven.

To serve

Place some potato in the centre of each plate.

Place an ox cheek on top of the potato, some spinach on the ox cheek, and a tomato on top of the spinach. Spoon some morel cream around the plate. Top with hollandaise and herbed breadcrumbs. Place some braised carrots on each plate and serve immediately.

Serves 4

4 ox cheeks, well trimmed
salt and freshly ground black pepper
1 tablespoon olive oil
200 ml red wine
6 shallots, peeled and roughly chopped
6 cloves garlic, peeled and crushed
2 sprigs rosemary
2 sprigs thyme
1½ litres chicken stock (see page 166)
50 g butter
100 g morel mushrooms
500 ml cream
1 recipe hollandaise sauce (see page 91)
1 recipe rosemary mashed potatoes (see page 121)
1 recipe crispy spinach (see page 125)
1 recipe roast shallots
1small bunch chives, finely chopped
1 recipe braised carrots (see page 90)
½ recipe overnight baked tomatoes (see page 127)
1 recipe herbed crumbs (see page 91)

Roast Shallots

These are delicious as an accompaniment to most meat dishes or sauces. They're like a fancier version of fried onions. The end result should be beautifully tender shallots with a rich buttery and caramel flavour.

Method

Heat the olive oil in a large frying pan. Add the shallots, butter and sugar. Cook gently for 10–15 minutes until the sugar starts to caramelise and the shallots take on a rich golden colour. Gradually add the chicken stock, allowing each addition to become absorbed before adding more.

Season with salt and serve immediately, or reheat as necessary with some extra butter.

Serves 4

1 tablespoon olive oil
16 shallots
30 g butter
30 g sugar
100 ml chicken stock (see page 166)
salt

Braised Carrots

Method

Preheat the oven to 150°C/300°F/gas mark 2.

Heat the butter in a medium-sized saucepan and sweat the carrots for 5 minutes. Add the baby carrots and chicken stock and transfer to an ovenproof dish. Season lightly and cook for 10–15 minutes in the oven until tender. Serve immediately or reheat in a small saucepan with some extra butter.

Serves 4

30 g butter
4 carrots, peeled and turned
12 baby carrots, peeled
25 ml chicken stock (see page 166)
salt and freshly ground black pepper

Hollandaise Sauce

This sauce is best made to order but it can be kept warm in a bain marie for up to 15 minutes if necessary.

Method

Reduce the vinegar by half. Place the egg yolks in a bain marie over a gentle heat and whisk with a small amount of butter and salt. When the yolk starts to thicken, gradually add more butter allowing each addition of butter to become incorporated before adding more. Add a little vinegar reduction and continue stirring in the butter. Taste and season if necessary. Keep warm in the bain marie for 10–15 minutes.

Serves 4
3 tablespoons white wine vinegar
2 egg yolks
100 g unsalted butter, diced
salt

Herbed Breadcrumbs

Method

Preheat the oven to 100°C/200°F/gas mark ½.

Process all the ingredients together on the pulse button. Lay out on a baking sheet and dry out in a warm oven for 10–15 minutes. Use as required.

Yields 75g
50 g dried breadcrumbs
1 teaspoon basil
1 teaspoon coriander
1 teaspoon chervil
1 teaspoon parsley
1 clove garlic, peeled and crushed
salt and freshly ground black pepper

Wine Suggestion

A big, soft red is the natural accompaniment for the smooth, open flavours of this French provincial dish. A southern Italian or New World red will work nicely. But a contrarian choice may be even better, so try putting a wine with real structure against the extremely tender ox cheeks. Côte Rôtie from the Côte Blonde of the northern Rhône, blended with white viognier, will counterpoint the morel cream. Barolo, which in its traditional forms tends to be lean and powerful, will balance the soft flavours of the beef. Good Burgundy, including wines as rich as Richebourg or Échézeaux, will also do well.

Herb-crusted Loin of Lamb with Chargrilled Aubergine, Goats' Cheese and Aubergine Purée

Herb-crusted Loin of Lamb with Chargrilled Aubergine, Goats' Cheese and Aubergine Purée

A smooth merging of the flavours of aubergine, cheese and lamb.

Method

Preheat the oven to 200°C/400°F/gas mark 6.

Heat 2 tablespoons of olive oil and fry the aubergine slices until golden on both sides. Set aside.

Heat another tablespoon of olive oil and the butter in a saucepan and sauté the red onions until soft, but do not allow them to colour.

Add the roasted red peppers and cabbage, and continue to cook until the cabbage starts to wilt. Add the goats' cheese and stir. Season and set aside.

Mix together the breadcrumbs, herbs and garlic. Season well and set aside. Smear the lamb loins with another tablespoon of olive oil, season well.

Heat the last tablespoon of olive oil in a frying pan and sear the loins on all sides. Coat the seared loins in the herbed breadcrumbs, transfer to a roasting tin and finish cooking in the oven for 5–7 minutes.

To serve

Reheat the aubergine slices in the oven. Gently heat the lamb jus and add the spring onions and chives. Reheat the goats' cheese mixture and the aubergine purée. Remove the lamb from the oven and leave to rest for 1 minute before carving.

Arrange an aubergine slice in the centre of each plate and place some of the goats' cheese mixture on top. Carve the lamb into thin slices and place on top of the goats' cheese mixture in a fan shape. Spoon some lamb jus over the plate and garnish with aubergine purée, aubergine chips and sprigs of thyme. Serve immediately.

Serves 4

5 tablespoons olive oil
½ aubergine, sliced into 4 equal rounds
30 g butter
2 red onions, peeled and finely chopped
4 roasted red peppers, cut into strips
½ Savoy cabbage, shredded
120 g goats' cheese
salt and freshly ground black pepper
100 g dried breadcrumbs
2 teaspoons parsley, finely chopped
2 teaspoons chervil, finely chopped
2 cloves garlic, peeled and crushed
2 lamb loins, well trimmed
150 ml lamb jus (see page 87)
8 spring onions, roughly chopped
1 small bunch chives, roughly chopped
1 recipe aubergine purée (see page 94)

Garnishes

4 aubergine chips (see page 125)
4 sprigs thyme

Aubergine Purée

Method

Preheat the oven to 140°C/275°F/gas mark 1.

Cut the aubergine in half lengthways. Make criss-cross cuts in the flesh, but do not cut through the skin. Insert the garlic, thyme, and fennel seeds into the cuts.

Place the aubergine on a sheet of tinfoil. Drizzle with half the olive oil and season with salt and pepper. Loosely wrap in the tinfoil and bake for 45 minutes.

Remove the aubergine from the oven and unwrap the foil (be careful of steam escaping). When the aubergine is cool enough to handle, discard the thyme. Scoop out the flesh and blend thoroughly, adding the remaining olive oil until you have a firm, not runny consistency. Adjust the seasoning.

Serve warm or allow to cool and reheat in a saucepan with some extra olive oil.

Serves 4
2 aubergines
1 garlic clove, peeled and sliced
2 sprigs thyme
1 teaspoon fennel seeds
100 ml olive oil
salt and freshly ground white pepper

Wine Suggestion

This will go nicely with a New World cabernet or merlot. Lots of other red varietals will work, from South African pinotage to Canadian pinot noir. An exceptional Australian red such as Grange will also do very well. But the classic marriage of flavours is with the Médoc, a cru bourgeois if needs be, but best of all a Pauillac or St Julien. The top Bordeaux chateau wines in the best vintages are extremely expensive, but some good and less expensive wines were made in unfashionable years such as 1983, 1987 and 1993.

Roast Squab with Spiced Lentils, Polenta Cakes and Creamed Cabbage with Caramelised Cranberries and Carrot and Ginger Sauce

Fledgling pigeon has fewer of the dark, gamey flavours of mature wild pigeon. Here, it gets a Christmas season flavour with cranberries and foie gras.

Method

Preheat the oven to 200°C/400°F/gas mark 6.

Remove the legs from the squabs. Season the legs and carcasses with salt and pepper. Heat 1 tablespoon of olive oil in a large frying pan and sear the legs and carcasses until they are evenly coloured. Transfer to a roasting tin. Finish cooking in the oven for 10–15 minutes, depending on how rare you want the birds.

Melt half the butter in a small saucepan and add the sugar. Cook for 2 minutes over a gentle heat and add the cranberries. Transfer to an ovenproof dish and bake for 5–10 minutes until very tender.

Heat the remaining butter and the cream in a medium-sized saucepan. Add the cabbage and season well. Cook gently until the cabbage is tender. Heat a tablespoon of olive oil in a frying pan. Fry the polenta cakes on both sides until crisp and golden. Transfer to the oven to keep warm. In separate saucepans, gently reheat the carrot and ginger sauce and the spiced lentils. Remove the squabs from the oven and leave to rest for 1 minute.

Heat the remaining olive oil in a frying pan. Sear the foie gras for 30 seconds on each side.

To serve

Place a polenta cake in the centre of each plate. Place a ring on top of the polenta cake, pile some spiced lentils in the ring, and then some creamed cabbage on top of the lentils. Pat down. Carefully remove the rings.

Remove the breasts from the squab and place on top of the cabbage. Top each breast with a slice of foie gras and spoon some carrot and ginger sauce around the dish. Arrange some cranberries on each dish and serve immediately.

Serves 4

2 squabs
salt and freshly ground black pepper
3 tablespoons olive oil
60 g butter
3 tablespoons sugar
50 g cranberries
50 ml cream
½ Savoy cabbage, shredded
4 polenta cakes (see page 118)
1 recipe carrot and ginger sauce (see page 96)
1 recipe spiced lentils (see page 116)

Garnish

4 slices foie gras

Carrot and Ginger Sauce

The ginger gives a great kick to this creamy sauce. When first processed it looks very thick, but after sieving it becomes much more liquid.

Method

Sweat the carrots and shallots in the olive oil for 10 minutes. Then add the ginger and butter. Continue to cook gently, then add the garlic, saffron and sugar. Season well with salt and pepper.

Turn the heat up and gradually add the stock. Simmer for 5–10 minutes, then add the cream.

Allow to cool slightly and blend. Pass through a fine sieve and pour into a clean saucepan.

Put the sauce back on the heat and simmer gently to reduce slightly. It should have the consistency of thick cream. Only then should you adjust the seasoning. Gently reheat as necessary.

Wine Suggestion

Young pigeon with spices, cranberries and a foie gras garnish could spell disaster for insipid wines, so this requires some big guns. In general, any well-made Bordeaux or Rhône syrah will have enough tannic structure and length to deal with the pigeon, but the sweet-and-sour flavours of the caramelised cranberries may do better with a softer style of red. Try a Californian zinfandel, or a rich Amarone from Valpolicella. New World shiraz, especially Australian, may also complement the carrot and ginger sauce. A soft merlot, from Chile or California, will also work.

Serves 4

4 carrots, peeled and sliced
10 shallots, peeled and finely chopped
1 tablespoon olive oil
6 cm piece root ginger, peeled and finely sliced
30 g butter
1 clove garlic, peeled and crushed
pinch of saffron
1 teaspoon sugar
salt and freshly ground white pepper
200 ml chicken stock (see page 166)
50 ml cream

PEACOCK ALLEY LIGHT

Peacock Alley's Caesar Salad

The addition of anchovies and egg yolk give this version of a famous American dish the authentic touch.

Everyone has their own way of making a good Caesar Salad. We serve crispy green leaves of cos lightly dressed, accompanied by little croutons of bread topped with anchovy and sage parcels. Anchovies are not everyone's favourite, so we keep their presence in the dressing to a minimum, but make up for it in the garnish using fresh anchovies instead of tinned ones.

Method

To make the dressing place all the ingredients in a food processor and process until smooth. Refrigerate and mix well before serving.

Preheat the oven to 150°C/300°F/gas mark 2. Heat the deep fat fryer to 180°C/350°F.

Break up the cos lettuce into individual leaves. Using an 8 cm pastry cutter cut the leaves into perfect circles. Wrap with damp paper towel and refrigerate until ready to use. Bake the slices of French bread until crisp. Sandwich an anchovy in between two sage leaves. Deep-fry until a light golden brown. Drain on kitchen paper. Place a parcel onto each crouton. Keep warm in the oven.

Toss the cos in the dressing, and add the Parmesan. Season with freshly ground black pepper, and then pile the leaves high onto each plate. Garnish with Parmesan shavings, and place two of the French bread slices onto each plate. Serve immediately.

Wine Suggestion

This calls for an assertive wine. A grassy New Zealand sauvignon blanc will not be overwhelmed, nor will a good rosé from Provence. A more unusual selection would be Greek white, a dry wine from Crete—or, more controversially, a retsina, which will have the resinous, oily attack to handle these strong flavours. An easier choice for this quintessentially American dish would be a cool-climate chardonnay from Oregon or British Columbia in Canada.

Serves 4

Dressing
110 ml olive oil
30 ml balsamic vinegar
1 egg yolk (optional)
2 cloves garlic, peeled
1 shallot, peeled and roughly chopped
1 teaspoon basil, roughly chopped
2 tablespoons Parmesan, finely grated
2 tinned anchovies, roughly chopped
salt and freshly ground black pepper
2 tablespoons warm water

2–3 heads of cos lettuce, outer leaves discarded
8 slices French bread
8 fresh anchovies, boned or 8 tinned anchovies
16 sage leaves
3 tablespoons Parmesan, finely grated
freshly ground black pepper
vegetable oil

Garnish
Parmesan shavings

Roasted Duck Breasts with Sweet Potato Purée, Red Onion Marmalade and Sauce Béarnaise

Sweet potato purée, onion marmalade and sauce béarnaise provide a rich accompaniment to the duck.

In Peacock Alley, we usually serve more than the three garnishes listed below. The duck ends up an amazing tower of sweet potato pont neuf, sweet potato purée, onion marmalade, crispy onions, sauté spinach and sauce béarnaise!

Method

Preheat the oven to 200°C/400°F/gas mark 6.

Gently reheat the sweet potato purée, onion marmalade and keep the sauce béarnaise warm in a bain marie.

Heat the olive oil and season the duck breasts with salt and freshly ground black pepper. Sear the duck breasts skin side down until golden brown. Do not be tempted to hurry this process as the duck fat must render down and start to caramelise. Drizzle the honey over the duck breasts and turn over to sear on the other side.

Serves 4

1 recipe sweet potato purée (see page 100)
1 recipe onion marmalade (see page 100)
1 recipe sauce béarnaise (see page 101)
2 tablespoons olive oil
4 duck breasts, skin on
salt and freshly ground black pepper
2 tablespoons honey

Sweet Potato Purée

The amount of stock and cream needed to make the purée depends on what equipment you use to purée the potatoes. A food processor or blender may over-activate the starch making the sweet potato too thick and stodgey. We use a very strong hand mixer which purées the potatoes without overworking them. You can use a food processor, but do so with care using the pulse button. If the texture is too thick, place the purée in a saucepan and add more stock and cream until you have the desired consistency. If the texture is too runny reduce the purée over a gentle heat until it thickens slightly. The end texture should be slightly thicker than other vegetable purées.

Serve 4
4 tablespoons olive oil
8 sweet potatoes, peeled and roughly chopped
100 g butter
200 ml chicken stock (see page 165)
200 ml cream
1 sprig thyme
salt and freshly ground black pepper

Method
Preheat the oven to 150°C/300°F/gas mark 2.

Heat the olive oil in a large saucepan and sweat the potatoes for 5 minutes. Do not allow to take on any colour.

Add the butter and cook for a further minute and then gradually add the chicken stock. Increase the heat, bring to the boil, then add the cream. Transfer to an ovenproof dish and cook for 25 minutes or until the potatoes are very tender.

Process with enough of the cooking liquor to make a purée. Pass through a fine sieve and adjust the seasoning. Reheat as required.

Sauce Béarnaise

A béarnaise sauce derives from the mother sauce—hollandaise (see page 91). It is best made to order but can be kept warm in a bain marie for up to 15 minutes if necessary.

Method

Place the vinegar, peppercorns and shallot in a small saucepan and reduce to about a tablespoon of vinegar. Strain and set aside.

Place the egg yolks in a bowl over a bain marie and season. Add a few cubes of butter and beat with a wooden spoon. When the butter has been incorporated and you notice the mixture thickening, add half the vinegar reduction and some more butter. Allow each addition of butter to become incorporated before adding more. Continue this process until nearly all the butter has been used. Check the seasoning and add more vinegar reduction if necessary.

Keep warm in the bain marie for up to 20 minutes, beating in the last piece of butter and herbs just before serving.

Wine Suggestion

This calls for a good aromatic white rather than a gamey red. Try instead a German auslese or an Austrian riesling—or something from Alsace, Silvaner or a white Muscat. Well-made French chardonnay will also work. If you prefer red wine, try a big, oaked Australian shiraz, or one of the powerful reds of the Bandol region of Provence.

Garnishes 4 main courses
50 ml tarragon vinegar
3 black peppercorns
½ shallot, peeled and roughly chopped
3 egg yolks
salt and freshly ground black pepper
150 g unsalted butter, cubed
2 teaspoons tarragon, finely chopped
1 teaspoon chervil, finely chopped

Marinated Chicken on Focaccia with Herbs, Goats' Cheese and Rocket

Simple country flavours of chicken married with focaccia are given a touch of sharpness and distinction by goats' cheese, tarragon, garlic and lemon juice

Focaccia bread is good for this style of rustic sandwich, but it would work equally well with any strongly flavoured bread.

Method

Marinate the chicken breasts in three-quarters of the olive oil, all of the tarragon and 1 clove of garlic for a few hours, or overnight.

Preheat the oven to 200°C/400°F/gas mark 6. Mix the remaining olive oil and garlic together with some black pepper and brush the slices of focaccia with it. Lightly toast.

Place the goats' cheese, chopped herbs and lemon juice in a food processor and process until smooth. Season with black pepper. Heat two tablespoons of the chicken marinade in a large frying pan and sear the chicken breasts on both sides until golden brown. Transfer to a baking tray and finish cooking in the oven for approximately 7–10 minutes. Reheat the overnight baked tomatoes and focaccia in the oven. Toss the rocket in the ginger and basil vinaigrette.

To serve

Slice the chicken breasts and then lay out 4 slices of focaccia. Layer up the rocket, overnight baked tomatoes, sliced chicken and cheese mixture. Top with the remaining slices of focaccia and slice diagonally. Serve immediately.

Wine Suggestion

A dish to stand up to robust wines, from Sicilian and Portuguese reds to spicy southern French syrah. Good Burgundy, from Savigny-lès-Beaune, Mercurey or Volnay, should also have enough of the farmyard on the nose to complement the goats' cheese and other ingredients. In Bordeaux, some of the dark, primarily merlot and cabernet franc, wines from Bourg and Blaye could be interesting. But the best matches could be Italian reds, Barbaresco or Chianti Classico. Interesting rustic reds are also emerging from Argentina in malbec, tempranillo blends.

Serves 4

4 chicken breasts, skin removed
225 ml olive oil
1 tablespoon tarragon, finely chopped
2 cloves garlic, peeled and crushed
salt and freshly black pepper
8 slices focaccia bread (see page 127)
200 g goats' cheese
2 tablespoons chopped herbs (e.g. basil, tarragon, chives)
2 tablespoons lemon juice
1 recipe overnight baked tomatoes (see page 127)
100 g rocket
½ recipe ginger and basil vinaigrette (see page 170)

Irish Breakfast in Manhattan

A triumphant way to begin a day on either side of the Atlantic—
black pudding with eggs, pancetta, grilled mushrooms and
pumpkin risotto

This dish was inspired by Seán James who owns Irish Food Distributors, a company that specialises in importing Irish produce into New York. We were discussing the merits of a traditional Irish breakfast, and decided it could do with being made a little more cosmopolitan. The result was this completely decadent dish that gives a new meaning to the word 'breakfast'.

Instead of adding the egg yolk to the risotto, you could poach 4 eggs and gently place one on top of each portion of risotto when serving.

Serves 4

1 recipe pumpkin risotto, (see
*   page 114)*
2 tablespoons olive oil
2 Irish black puddings, sliced
*   diagonally into 2 cm slices*
50 g butter
12 slices pancetta
8 black trumpet mushrooms
1 teaspoon balsamic vinegar
salt and freshly ground black
*   pepper*
4 egg yolks

Method

Prepare the risotto for finishing at the last minute.

Preheat the oven to 150°C/300°F/gas mark 2, preheat grill to high setting.

Heat the olive oil in a large saucepan and fry the black pudding on both sides until crisp on the outside. Keep warm in the oven. Grill the pancetta on both sides until crisp. Keep warm in the oven.

Melt the butter in a large frying pan, and sauté the mushrooms for a few minutes. Add the balsamic vinegar and then season lightly. Transfer to the oven to keep warm.

Finish off the risotto and add the egg yolks. Heat through and then divide the risotto, black pudding, pancetta and mushrooms between each plate. Serve immediately.

Wine Suggestion

Preferably, do this the traditional way with Irish breakfast tea—or better still, a more aromatic Earl Grey. Spike the tea with Irish whiskey if you want to be decadent. Good coffee, including espresso, will also be fine. But if it is a late breakfast or brunch and alcohol is in order, champagne and orange juice will do the trick. If the champagne is good, spare the orange and drink the bubbles.

Warm Salmon Salad with Fennel, Artichokes and Sauté Sweet Potatoes

Lightly cooked salmon makes an elegantly simple dish with artichokes, fennel and the sturdy flavours of walnut oil, sherry vinegar and Dijon mustard.

This is a great dish for a spring or summer lunch or dinner. You could also poach the salmon and serve the salad cold, or barbecue the salmon and serve with hot sauté potatoes and the salad.

If you can't find fresh artichokes use good-quality tinned artichoke hearts. Make sure to drain them really well before mixing with the other ingredients. Serve the sauté potatoes hot or cold.

Method

Remove the skin from the salmon. Run your fingers against the grain of the fish and remove any pin bones with tweezers. Refrigerate until ready to cook.

Break off the stalk of the artichoke. Trim the base and remove all the outer leaves until only the heart is left. You can remove the choke at this stage, or remove it with a teaspoon after cooking. Rub the hearts with a lemon half to help prevent them discolouring. Add half the lemon juice to a saucepan of boiling salted water and blanch the hearts for 15 to 20 minutes or until tender. Drain and sprinkle with the remaining lemon juice. Quarter them and set aside to cool.

Remove the feathery tips and outer leaves from the fennel, chop them roughly and set aside. Slice the fennel bulbs very finely and mix with the artichokes and tomatoes. Set aside.

Blend the chives, walnut oil, sherry vinegar and mustard. Season well and pour over the artichoke salad.

Heat the olive oil in a large frying pan. Season the salmon with salt and pepper and fry for about 2 minutes on each side, along with the fennel trimmings. Discard the fennel trimmings when the salmon is cooked. Cook the salmon a little longer if you like it well done.

To serve

Place some salad on each plate and garnish with overlapping slices of sauté sweet potato. Top with a salmon fillet and serve immediately.

Serves 4
4 x 120 g salmon fillets
8 globe artichokes or 8 tinned globe artichoke hearts
juice of 3 lemons
freshly ground black pepper
2 heads fennel
4 plum tomatoes, skinned, deseeded and finely chopped or 4 overnight baked tomatoes (see page 127)
1 small bunch chives, finely chopped
3 tablespoons walnut oil
1 tablespoon sherry vinegar
1 teaspoon Dijon mustard
salt and freshly ground black pepper
2 tablespoons olive oil
1 recipe sauté sweet potatoes (see page 105)

Sauté Sweet Potatoes

Method

Preheat the oven to 200°C/400°F/gas mark 6.

Cut the sweet potatoes into slices 2 cm thick. Heat the butter in a frying pan and fry the potatoes on both sides until golden.

Add the stock, garlic and rosemary. Season to taste. Cook for a few minutes, allowing most of the stock to evaporate, and then transfer to a roasting tin and cook in the oven for about 10 minutes or until tender.

Serves 4

3 large sweet potatoes, unpeeled
50 g butter
100 ml chicken or vegetable stock (see page 166/7)
1 clove garlic, peeled and thinly sliced
2 sprigs rosemary
salt and freshly ground black pepper

Wine Suggestion

A dry white Rully from Burgundy, or a white Vouvray, should work with the salmon and artichokes, but the walnut oil, mustard and other ingredients call for something with more ability to handle spicy, nutty flavours. A pinot gris or pinot blanc, from Italy, Alsace or Hungary, should stand up well. Australian producers are also developing a dry but fruity style of riesling that makes it very interesting with complex food.

A Tart of Polenta with Red Onion, Fennel and Red Pepper Purée

Anchovies and lemon juice give this dish a salty tartness, offset by the eggs and polenta and the caramelised notes of fennel, leeks and red pepper.

This filling is really delicious—the egg and cream topping adds an extra richness, without giving the tart the rubbery quality often associated with quiches. The trick is not to overcook the eggs—10 minutes is plenty of time to just set and colour the topping. Remember, the heat from the filling will continue to cook the topping when it's removed from the oven. The filling can be made well in advance, but it is important to reheat it before filling the pastry cases. The tart only cooks for 5–10 minutes which is not long enough to heat the filling if it is taken straight from the refrigerator.

Method

Preheat the oven to 190°C/375°F/gas mark 5.

Heat the butter and oil together in a medium-sized saucepan, and sweat the onions and fennel until starting to soften. Add the sugar and increase the heat slightly until the mixture starts to caramelise and then add the leeks, anchovies and red peppers. Season lightly with salt and plenty of pepper. Add the lemon juice, rosemary and garlic. Taste and set aside to cool slightly. Pour the red pepper purée into the pastry case or cases and smooth out.

Add the filling and gently smooth out. Whisk together the cream, eggs and Parmesan. Season and pour on top of the filling. Bake for 5–10 minutes. The topping should just start to set, but should not wobble too much.

Remove from the oven and allow to cool for 5 minutes before serving.

Serves 4

30 g butter
2 tablespoons olive oil
1 onion, peeled and finely sliced
3 red onions, peeled and finely sliced
1 fennel bulb, finely sliced
1 tablespoon sugar
4 leeks, white part only, finely sliced
8 anchovies, finely chopped
4 roasted red peppers, finely sliced (see page 128)
salt and freshly ground black pepper
juice of 1 lemon
2 sprigs rosemary, finely chopped
2 cloves garlic, peeled and crushed
½ recipe red pepper purée (see opposite)
1 recipe polenta pastry case or cases, baked blind (see page 47)
100 ml cream
2 eggs, beaten
50 g Parmesan, finely grated

Red Pepper Purée

Use this purée as an accompaniment to grilled chicken or fish. It can also be used to flavour bread or pasta, or to enhance a pasta sauce.

Method

Heat the olive oil in a large saucepan and sweat the shallots and garlic until soft. Add the butter, thyme and peppers and cook for a further 5 minutes over a gentle heat.

Turn the heat up and gradually add the vegetable stock. Reduce by half and season.

Remove from the heat and allow to cool slightly. Purée in a blender or food processor and strain. Refrigerate until ready to use. The purée will keep overnight.

Wine Suggestion

Anchovies make for a difficult food match. A young, light Italian red, or one of Portugal's vinho verde whites, will work, or perhaps a Provencal rosé. A soft New World merlot from Chile or California may also act in discreet counterpoint to these rich flavours.

Serves 4
30 ml olive oil
2 shallots, peeled and finely chopped
1 clove garlic, peeled and crushed
30 g butter
2 sprigs thyme
4 red peppers, roughly chopped
500 ml vegetable stock (see page 167)
salt and freshly ground black pepper

Crabmeat Salad with Avocado Cream, Summer Vegetables and Pink Grapefruit

Avocados and crème fraîche bring a plump, rounded touch to crabmeat salad, counterbalanced with the citrus notes of lemon and grapefruit.

Pictured on page 97, this is the summer version of the crabmeat salad with beetroot. It has a very simple and clean taste and is very easy to make.

Method

Flake the crabmeat into a bowl and discard any bone and filament. Mix with the crème fraîche, lemon juice and herbs. Season well and chill until ready to serve. Prepare the summer vegetables: mix three-quarters of the lemon grass vinaigrette with the carrots and turnip. Season well and allow to marinate for 10 minutes.

To serve

Place a ring or pastry cutter in the centre of each plate and spoon equal amounts of the summer vegetables into each ring. Spoon a layer of crabmeat on top, and then a layer of avocado cream. Carefully remove the ring and garnish with the pink grapefruit and sprigs of mint. Drizzle the plates with the remaining vinaigrette and serve immediately.

Serves 4
400 g cooked crabmeat
3 tablespoons crème fraîche
2 tablespoons lemon juice
2 teaspoons mint, finely chopped
1 teaspoon tarragon, finely chopped
salt and freshly ground black pepper
1 recipe lemon grass vinaigrette (see page 170)
2 carrots, peeled and very finely sliced
2 white turnips, peeled and very finely diced
1 recipe avocado cream (see below)
8 segments pink grapefruit
4 sprigs mint

Avocado Cream

Method

Halve the avocados and remove the stone. Scrape out the flesh into a food processor and add the crème fraîche and half the lemon juice. Process until smooth and season well.

Transfer into a bowl and pour the remaining lemon juice onto the surface of the avocado cream. Chill until ready to serve. Before serving mix in the lemon juice.

Serves 4
2 large avocados
2 tablespoons crème fraîche
juice of 2 lemons
salt and freshly ground pepper

Wine Suggestion

A good Chablis from the excellent 1995 vintage will have the lemony zest to do well. A traditional chardonnay from Burgundy proper, a Meursault, for example, is also an elegant choice. Chilean or New Zealand chardonnay will also work, and there are surprisingly good expressions of the most popular white grape in countries like Canada and in Washington State in the United States.

PASTA, GRAINS AND PULSES

Ravioli of Winter Greens and Langoustines with Carrot and Ginger Sauce

Langoustines make an expensive but interesting garnish for ravioli stuffed with vegetables.

This dish would suit vegetarians, provided you make the carrot and ginger sauce with vegetable stock. Add anything you like to the filling—some goats' cheese or seared langoustines. How many langoustines you serve depends entirely on your budget. In Peacock Alley we also drizzle some ginger oil over the ravioli and serve it with slices of Périgord truffle.

Method

To make the filling, melt 20 g of the butter in a medium-sized saucepan and sweat a quarter each of the red pepper, the tomatoes and the spinach, reserving the remaining three-quarters for the base.

Add the lemon rind/zest, pesto and half the chopped basil leaves. Season well and mix. Allow to cool fully before stuffing the ravioli.

Roll out the pasta using a pasta machine or rolling pin. Divide the sheet into two rectangles. Keep one sheet covered with a clean tea towel or clingfilm while you work with the other.

Using 8 cm (4 inch) and 12 cm (5 inch) pastry cutters, cut out four discs of each size. Place two tablespoons of cold filling in the centre of each smaller disc and top with a larger disc.

Seal the edges, using a dampened finger if the pasta has become too dry. Try to get rid of any air pockets when sealing the ravioli. Cover and set aside.

You could make and stuff the ravioli the day before. Blanch them for a minute and refresh under cold water. Drizzle with some olive oil and keep well wrapped in clingfilm until ready to use. Reheat in a saucepan with some boiling water or chicken stock and proceed as below.

Preheat the grill to a high setting.

To make the base, heat 40 g butter in a medium-sized frying pan

Serves 4
150 g butter
2 roasted red peppers, skinned and cut into strips (see page 128)
4 tomatoes, skinned, deseeded and finely chopped (see page 176)
225 g baby spinach, chopped
zest of 2 lemons
1 tablespoon basil pesto (see page 115)
1 tablespoon basil leaves, chopped
salt and freshly ground black pepper
¼ recipe pasta dough (see page 113)
1 bunch spring onions, chopped
2 leeks, white part only, chopped
3 tablespoons olive oil
20 g Parmesan, grated
110 g pumpkin purée (see page 115)
1 recipe carrot and ginger sauce (see page 96)

Garnishes
4–12 langoustines (optional)

Risotto with Pumpkin Purée or Basil and Rocket Pesto

In Peacock Alley we flavour creamy risotto with pumpkin in the winter and pesto in t he summer.

When making risotto be sure to use good-quality rice (arborio, carnaroli or vialoni) and a good stock. After that you can add almost anything. In Peacock Alley we usually flavour risotto with cream, mascarpone and Parmesan adding pumpkin purée or basil and rocket pesto to vary it. Sometimes we substitute pearl barley for the risotto rice, and flavour the risotto with pesto or sundried tomatoes. Here we describe how to prepare the risotto for serving immediately, and we also give a method for preparing it in advance, to be finished off just before serving.

Method

Place the stock in a saucepan, bring to the boil and set aside.

Sweat the shallot in the butter for about 2 minutes in a medium-sized saucepan, but do not allow it to colour. Season lightly. Add the rice and stir well, coating it with butter, for about 1 minute (again, do not allow to take on any colour). Gradually add the hot stock, stirring constantly and adding more stock only when the previous addition has been absorbed. Continue until all the stock is absorbed.

Meanwhile, in a small saucepan, gently heat the cream, mascarpone, Parmesan and pumpkin purée or pesto. Allow to reduce slightly and add to the risotto as soon as it's ready. Quickly stir and serve immediately. The whole process should take 20–25 minutes.

If you are preparing the risotto in advance, use only 450 ml of the stock and, after about 10 minutes, remove it from the heat and spread the mixture on a baking tray. Allow to cool fully, then cover and set aside until ready to finish. To finish cooking prepare the cream mixture as above, and reheat the stock. Return the risotto to a clean saucepan over gentle heat and repeat the process of gradually adding the remaining hot stock. After about 3–4 minutes the risotto should be cooked, but still *al dente*. Add the cream mixture. Quickly stir and serve immediately.

Serves 4

600 ml chicken or vegetable stock (see page 166/7)
1 shallot, peeled and finely chopped
30 g butter
salt and freshly ground black pepper
200 g risotto rice (arborio, carnaroli or vialoni) or 200 g pearl barley
1 tablespoon cream
1 tablespoon mascarpone
20 g Parmesan, grated
6 tablespoons pumpkin purée (see opposite) or 3 tablespoons basil and rocket pesto (see opposite)

Pumpkin Purée

There is a huge amount of butter in this recipe, but that gives it a super-rich quality. Most of the time we add it to potatoes or risottos. However, if you are using it on its own, use less butter. If you can't get pumpkin, you can use squash—if you are really stuck, use carrots.

Method

Heat the olive oil and butter in a medium-sized saucepan, add the pumpkin flesh and season well.

Cook over a gentle heat for around 10–15 minutes, without allowing the pumpkin to colour. Turn up the heat and add small quantities of vegetable stock, which will deglaze the pan. As the vegetable stock reduces, gradually add more. You're trying to achieve a very soft but quite dry mixture.

Process until smooth in a blender or food processor. You may have to add some water or vegetable stock to help process the purée, but it will evaporate when you reheat it.

Season well with salt and pepper. Reheat as necessary with some butter over a gentle heat.

1 tablespoon olive oil
50 g butter
250 g pumpkin/squash flesh, peeled and diced
250 ml vegetable stock (see page 167)
salt and freshly ground white pepper

Basil, or Basil and Rocket, Pesto

Method

Place the basil, garlic, pine nuts and Parmesan in a food processor with approximately 50 ml olive oil. Blend and gradually add the remaining oil until you have the desired consistency. Season well with salt and black pepper. To make basil and rocket pesto substitute 25 g of rocket for 25 g of the basil.

50 g basil leaves or 25g basil and 25 g rocket leaves
6 garlic cloves, peeled
50 g pine nuts
125 g Parmesan, grated
175 ml olive oil
salt and freshly ground black pepper

Wine suggestion

Risotto is a wonderfully flexible dish with wine, and here the rich ingredients and creaminess allow you to go to town. Northern Italian wines are the traditional accompaniment—a younger, modern style of Barolo rather than the tannic traditional style. A very rich wine like Amarone will have the softness and huge alcohol hit to round out the dish, as would a 'super Tuscan' such as Tignanello. Many good white wines will also work well.

Spiced Lentils

Puy lentils are grown in the volcanic soils of Velay in France, where they obtain a beautiful marbled deep green colour and distinctive flavour. It is always best to pick over the lentils before rinsing and soaking them, as they can camouflage small stones.

Method

Place the lentils in a sieve and rinse well. Transfer to a large bowl and cover with water. Soak for 2 hours and then drain.

Heat the olive oil in a large saucepan and sauté the shallots with the garlic and ginger. Add the balsamic vinegar, soy sauce and sugar. Pour the lentils on top and mix well. Tie the rosemary and thyme together, or wrap in some muslin, and place in the middle of the lentils. Add enough stock to cover and simmer gently for an hour, adding more stock if it evaporates too quickly

Season the lentil mixture, remove it from the heat, and pour into a large roasting tin. This will help the lentils to cool quickly and will also enable you to remove the shallots, garlic, ginger, and herbs easily. Reheat as necessary before serving.

Serves 4

1 tablespoon olive oil
5 shallots, peeled
5 cloves garlic, peeled
25 g root ginger, peeled and cut into quarters
1 tablespoon balsamic vinegar
2 tablespoons soy sauce
1 teaspoon sugar
200 g Puy lentils
3 sprigs rosemary
3 sprigs thyme
400 ml chicken stock (see page 166)
salt and freshly ground black pepper

Polenta with Two Cheeses

Polenta is very versatile, as it goes, and can be flavoured with just about everything. It is eaten largely in northern Italy, where it sometimes replaces bread at mealtimes. However, it needs to be well flavoured as it can be very bland if made with water and under-seasoned. Polenta can be further enriched by cooking it with a combination of milk and water or some cream added to the stock, and then finished off with a couple of beaten egg yolks when adding the mascarpone and Parmesan. Once you are confident about making polenta, you can create endless combinations to flavour it.

Method
Heat the butter and stock together in a heavy based medium sized saucepan. Bring to the boil and then reduce the heat until simmering.

Slowly add the polenta in a thin stream, stirring constantly with a wooden spoon. Once all the polenta has been added simmer gently on the lowest heat possible until the mixture is thick and comes away from the side of the pan. The mixture at the bottom of the saucepan will burn slightly. Just ignore this but don't try to incorporate it with the rest of the polenta. After about 45 minutes the polenta will lose the raw corn taste—it should have the texture of porridge. Stir frequently during cooking.

To serve
Add the two cheeses, cream, olive oil and butter and season lightly. Serve immediately.

Serves 4
30 g butter
1 litre chicken or vegetable stock (see page 166/167)
200 g fine polenta
2 tablespoons mascarpone
50 g Parmesan, grated
1 tablespoon cream
2 tablespoons olive oil
100 g butter
salt and freshly ground black pepper

Chilli Polenta

Method
Proceed exactly as above, but substituting 100 g chilli butter for the butter.

Serves 4
1 recipe polenta with two cheeses (see above)
100 g smoked chilli butter (see page 32)

Fennel Polenta

Method
Melt the butter and sauté the fennel bulb with some salt and pepper and the fennel seeds. When tender add to the Polenta with Two Cheeses along with the extra Parmesan.

Serves 4
½ fennel bulb, finely sliced
30 g butter
salt and pepper
½ teaspoon fennel seeds, crushed
1 recipe polenta with two cheeses (see page 117)
50 g Parmesan, grated

Polenta Cakes

The cakes can be shaped to suit your requirements. For garnishes we serve them slightly flat and cut into rectangular shapes but leave them thicker and cut into circular cakes when used as an accompaniment. They are also delicious topped with some tomato fondue (see page 49) and a little cheese and grilled for a few minutes for an alternative pizza.

Method
Add the chives to the cooked Polenta with Two Cheeses. Season lightly and transfer to a lightly oiled baking tray. Smooth out and cool for about an hour until set.

Cut into the desired shapes and shallow fry in the olive oil or brush both sides with the oil and grill until golden on both sides. Serve hot.

When adding the mascarpone, Parmesan and chives, you could also add sundried tomatoes and rosemary or tomatoes and basil.

Serves 4
1 recipe polenta with two cheeses (see page 117)
1 tablespoon chives, finely chopped
salt and freshly ground black pepper
3 tablespoons olive oil

Optional extras
40 g sundried tomatoes, finely chopped
1 tablespoon rosemary, finely chopped or 2 tomatoes, skinned, deseeded and finely chopped
1 tablespoon basil, finely chopped

Pesto Couscous

Couscous can be very bland, so make sure your stock is full of flavour. During the summer months this is delicious served with Grilled Mediterranean Vegetables (see page 126) and a green salad for a simple supper.

Method
Melt the butter in a medium sized saucepan. Add the couscous and cook for a minute over a gentle heat.

   Heat the stock to boiling point, add it to the couscous and stir in the pesto and lemon juice.

To serve
Season and serve or allow to cool and serve cold or reheat as necessary with some extra stock.

Serves 4
20 g butter
300 g couscous
300 ml chicken or vegetable stock (see page 166/7)
juice of 2 lemons
4 tablespoons basil pesto (see page 115)
salt and freshly ground black pepper

Sundried Tomato Couscous

Method
Make in exactly the same way as pesto couscous (above) but substitute 4 tablespoons of sundried tomato tapenade (see page 69) for the basil pesto.

VEGETABLE
DISHES

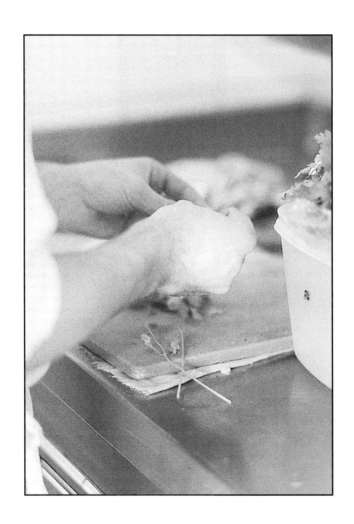

Vegetable Dishes

Basil Mashed Potatoes

Method

Heat the butter and cream and allow to reduce slightly. Add the chopped basil leaves and gradually stir in the mashed potatoes. Fold in the basil oil for extra flavour and colour and season with salt and pepper. Serve immediately.

To prepare in advance, cook the mashed potatoes and allow to cool. Make the butter and cream reduction and allow to cool. Just before serving, reheat together and season well.

Serves 4
50 g butter
50 ml cream
10 basil leaves, finely sliced
1 recipe mashed potatoes (see page 122)
20 ml basil oil (see page 168)
salt and freshly ground black pepper

Champ Potatoes

Method

Sweat the butter and spring onions together. Add the cream and reduce until thick.

Add the mashed potatoes to the spring onion mixture. Season well and serve immediately.

To prepare in advance, cook the mashed potatoes and allow to cool. Make the butter and cream reduction and allow it to cool. Just before serving, mix the two together, reheat and season well.

Serves 4
50 g butter
1 bunch of spring onions, finely chopped
50 ml cream
1 recipe mashed potatoes (see page 122)
salt and freshly ground black pepper

Rosemary and Goats' Cheese Mashed Potato

Goats' cheese is quite strong and can also be quite salty, so taste before seasoning very lightly with salt, if at all.

Method

Heat together the butter, cream and rosemary in a medium-sized saucepan. Reduce until the mixture is thick. Add the potatoes to this mixture and beat in the goats' cheese using a wooden spoon. Check seasoning and add a little salt if necessary and plenty of pepper.

To prepare in advance, cook the mashed potato and allow to cool. Make the butter and cream reduction and allow to cool. Just before serving reheat the two together, beat in the goats' cheese. Season and serve immediately.

Serves 4
50 g butter
50 ml cream
1 tablespoon rosemary, finely chopped
1 recipe mashed potatoes (see page 122)
30 g goats' cheese, roughly chopped
salt and freshly ground black pepper

Pumpkin Mashed Potato

Method
Heat the butter and cream. Add the pumpkin purée and then gradually add the mashed potato. Mix well and heat through. Season with salt and pepper and serve immediately.

Serves 4
50 g butter
50 ml cream
½ recipe pumpkin purée (see page 115)
1 recipe mashed potato (see below)
salt and freshly ground black pepper

Colcannon

There are many variations of Colcannon all over the world—this is the Peacock Alley version.

Method
Blanch the cabbage or kale in boiling salted water until tender but still crisp. Sweat the butter and spring onions in a large saucepan. Add the cream and reduce until thick. Add the mashed potatoes to the butter and cream reduction. Add the cabbage or kale and half the corned beef. Mix and season well. Serve immediately with the remaining slices of corned beef on top of the colcannon.

To prepare in advance, cook the mashed potatoes (see below) and allow to cool. Make the butter and cream reduction and allow to cool. Blanch the cabbage or kale and allow to cool. Just before serving, reheat the butter and cream reduction together with the mashed potatoes in a large saucepan. Add the cabbage or kale and half the corned beef and mix. Heat through. Season well and serve as above.

Serves 4
½ Savoy cabbage or kale, shredded
salt and freshly ground black pepper
50 g butter
3 spring onions
50 ml cream
1 recipe mashed potatoes (see below)
100 g corned beef, finely sliced

Mashed Potatoes

When mashing potatoes, do not be tempted to make life easier by mixing them in a food processor. The starch may overwork and the potatoes turn into a starchy, stodgy mound. On the other hand, if you have made a purée that is too runny, add some boiled potato to give the purée a firmer consistency.

Method
Place the potatoes in a large saucepan and cover with water. Bring to the boil, reduce the heat and simmer for approximately 20 minutes or until tender.

Drain and mash the potatoes and then pass through a sieve for an extra-smooth texture.

Serves 4
8 potatoes, peeled and cut into quarters

Ratatouille

Most ratatouille recipes contain either fresh or tinned tomatoes, which makes the dish similar to a stew. This recipe is quite dry; we use it mainly as a garnish, or served with some couscous.

Method

Heat the olive oil. Sweat the onion, aubergine, courgette and peppers until they start to soften. Add the garlic and sugar and season well.

In a separate saucepan heat the tomato purée and white wine. Mix well and add to the vegetables. Cook gently for about 15 minutes. Serve warm or cold.

Serves 4 as a garnish
2 tablespoons olive oil
1 red onion, peeled and diced
1 aubergine, diced
1 courgette, diced
1 red pepper, deseeded and finely sliced
1 yellow pepper, deseeded and finely sliced
1 green pepper, deseeded and finely sliced
2 cloves garlic, peeled and crushed
1 tablespoon sugar
salt and freshly ground black pepper
100 g tomato purée
70 ml white wine

Confit of Fennel

Method

Preheat the oven to 100°C/200°F/gas mark ½.

Pour 30 ml of the olive oil on to a large baking tray and sprinkle it with sea salt. Remove the feathery tips and the coarse part of the root from the fennel and discard. Slice the fennel lengthways.

Pour the lemon juice over the fennel, then sprinkle it with the zest, caraway seeds, thyme and pepper. Smear some greaseproof paper with the remaining olive oil and spread this over the fennel, oily side down. Bake for 45 minutes or until tender.

For a delicious side dish, allow one bulb per person and increase the other ingredients accordingly. Serve with Polenta with Two Cheeses (see page 117).

Garnishes 4 servings
40 ml olive oil
1 tablespoons coarse sea salt
1 fennel bulb
juice and zest of 1 lemon
½ tablespoon caraway seeds
1 sprig thyme
freshly ground black pepper

Chargrilled Leeks

Method

Preheat the oven to 180°C/350°F/gas mark 4.

Slice the leeks into 2 cm slices, angling the knife at 45 degrees. Brush with the olive oil and season lightly. Place a chargrill pan on a high heat. When the pan is very hot, arrange the leeks on the pan so that when you turn them over, they have a criss-cross pattern. When they are well charred on both sides, transfer them to an ovenproof dish and add the stock and the butter. Cook in the oven for about 5 minutes or until tender. Remove from the stock and serve immediately. The stock can be reused for soups or sauces.

Serves 4
4 large leeks, white part only
3 tablespoons olive oil
salt and freshly ground white pepper
200 ml vegetable stock (see page 167)
30 g butter

Chargrilled Aubergines

Method

Place a chargrill pan over a medium heat.

Slice the aubergine into 1½ cm rounds, making 4 rounds of similar size; the rest can be used for aubergine purée or to make large aubergine chips.

Brush both sides of the rounds with the olive oil and chargrill on both sides until tender. Season well and serve immediately or reheat in a warm oven as necessary.

Serves 4 as a garnish
1 medium aubergine
2 tablespoons olive oil
salt and freshly ground black pepper

Braised Salsify

Method

Heat the olive oil in a large saucepan and add the salsify. Sauté for about 1 minute and season well.

Add the sugar and butter. Cook until the sugar starts to caramelise and the salsify is beginning to turn golden brown. Turn the heat up and gradually add the stock, allowing each addition of stock to be absorbed before adding more.

Serve immediately or allow to cool and reheat with some extra butter over a gentle heat.

Serves 4
1 tablespoon olive oil
12–16 salsify, peeled and sliced lengthwise
salt and freshly ground black pepper
1 tablespoon sugar
50 g butter
400 ml vegetable or chicken stock (see page 166/7)

Confit of Garlic

The garlic is blanched three times before being poached in the hot fat. Using duck or goose fat will give a better flavour, but it is not absolutely necessary.

Method

Bring a small saucepan of water to the boil. Blanch the garlic for 1 minute, then remove from the water with a slotted spoon. Refresh the garlic under cold running water and transfer back into the boiling water to blanch again. Refresh the garlic once more and repeat this process a third time.

Meanwhile heat the fat in a small saucepan. The temperature should be about 90°C/195°F. Add the garlic and remaining ingredients and cook at a temperature of about 80°C/175°F for about 10 minutes. The garlic should be tender to the touch when cooked. It shouldn't take on too much colour—it's being poached, not fried, which would make it turn bitter. This slow soft cooking brings out the garlic's sweetness.

Serves 4
16 cloves garlic, unpeeled
vegetable oil, duck fat or goose fat
1 bay leaf
1 sprig rosemary
1 sprig thyme
4 black peppercorns

If you are using it immediately, drain on kitchen paper and serve, or allow to cool in the fat and transfer to the fridge, where it will keep for up to a week.

To reheat, simply transfer the garlic to a small saucepan with 2 tablespoons of the fat and gently heat through.

Sauté Cabbage

The sesame oil gives a distinctly Asian flavour to the cabbage which can be made even stronger by adding a little soy sauce just before serving.

Method
Heat both the oils in a large wok or a large saucepan. Add the cabbage and sauté for 2–3 minutes. Add the butter and season well with the salt or soy sauce and some pepper.

Gently mix, shaking the wok or saucepan. Continue to cook for another 2–3 minutes until the cabbage is tender. Serve immediately.

Serves 4
1 tablespoon sesame oil
1 tablespoon olive oil
1 large Savoy cabbage, shredded
30 g butter
salt or soy sauce
freshly ground black pepper

Crispy Spinach

The spinach isn't crispy as such, but it's cooked so quickly that it does retain a certain crispness. The quantity here is enough for a garnish, but you could double the quantities for a good supper dish which you could serve with some Colcannon (see page 122).

Method
Heat the olive oil in a medium-sized saucepan. Add the spinach leaves and butter and toss quickly. Season with salt and pepper and serve immediately.

Serves 4 as a garnish
½ tablespoon olive oil
100 g spinach, stalks removed
30 g butter
salt and freshly ground black pepper

Aubergine Chips

Method
Heat the oil to 130°C/250°F in a suitable pan or deep fat fryer. Fry the aubergine slices until golden brown and crispy.

Drain on kitchen paper and season with salt and freshly ground black pepper.

Serve immediately or cool fully and store in an airtight container. Reheat in a warm oven.

Serves 4 as a garnish
1 baby aubergine, sliced as thinly as possible
vegetable oil
salt and freshly ground black pepper

Grilled Mediterranean Vegetables

This is a good dish for a buffet, as it can be eaten hot or cold. Other vegetables to use would be plum tomatoes, spring onions and broccoli florets.

Method
Marinate the squash, courgettes and aubergine slices in the olive oil and freshly ground black pepper for at least an hour. Preheat the grill to its highest setting.

Remove the vegetables from the marinade and grill them until charred on both sides. Add the peppers at the last minute to heat through. Season with salt and plenty of pepper.

To serve
Arrange the vegetables on the plates and drizzle with some basil oil.

Serves 4
1 yellow squash, sliced into 2 cm rounds
2 courgettes, sliced into 2 cm rounds
1 aubergine, sliced into 2 cm rounds
100 ml olive oil
freshly ground black pepper
2 roasted red peppers, cut into strips (see page 128)
1 roasted yellow pepper, cut into strips (see page 128)
100 ml basil oil (see page 168)
salt

Beetroot Chips

Method
Peel and trim the beetroot until it is an even shape. Slice it as thinly as possible and blanch in boiling salted water for about 60 seconds. Drain and refresh under cold running water. Dry on kitchen paper.

Heat the oil in a suitable pan or deep fat fryer to 170°C/325°F and fry the slices until crisp. Remove with a slotted spoon and drain on kitchen paper. Season with salt and freshly ground black pepper.

Serve immediately or allow to cool completely and store in an airtight container until ready to use.

Serves 4 as a garnish
1 beetroot
salt
vegetable oil
freshly ground pepper

Roasted Parsnips

This recipe serves four as a substantial garnish. Double the quantity if you want to serve it as a side dish. You'll find it is so delicious that you may even have to treble the quantities.

Method
Preheat the oven to 200°C/400°F/gas mark 6.

Place all the ingredients in a roasting tin and cover with tinfoil. Roast for about 10 minutes, remove the foil, and continue to cook for a further 15–20 minutes. The parsnips should be tender and golden brown. Serve immediately.

Serves 4 as a garnish
4 parsnips, peeled and cut into batons
1 tablespoon olive oil
50 g butter
1 tablespoon honey
salt and freshly ground black pepper
1 clove garlic, peeled and crushed

Overnight Baked Tomatoes

Although tomatoes are strictly speaking a fruit vegetable, they are, along with aubergines and peppers, generally treated as vegetables. Ironically the tomato was originally thought to be toxic by the countries where it is now an indispensable part of the cuisine —Spain, Italy and France. These overnight baked tomatoes are absolutely delicious and best made with over-ripe tomatoes. They are used as garnishes in Peacock Alley but are equally good served with some crusty French bread to soak up all the delicious flavours.

Serves 4
20 g coarse sea salt
8 plum tomatoes, halved
8 tablespoons olive oil
4 shallots, peeled and chopped
4 cloves garlic, peeled and sliced
2 sprigs rosemary
2 sprigs thyme
20 g caster sugar

Method
Preheat the oven to 100°C/200°F/gas mark °.

Sprinkle sea salt on a large baking tray. Place the tomatoes, skin side up, on the salt. Pour the olive oil over the tomatoes and sprinkle the remaining ingredients on top. Bake overnight if possible, but for at least 6–8 hours—the tomatoes will look shrivelled but should keep their shape. Remove from the oven and allow to cool slightly before removing the skins. Reheat in a moderate oven.

Curried Matchstick Potatoes

These are a good accompaniment to Marinated Chicken on Focaccia (see page 102).

Serves 4
4–6 potatoes, peeled and cut into fine julienne strips
3 tablespoons curry powder
vegetable oil (for deep fat frying)
salt and freshly ground black pepper

Method
Place the potatoes in a large bowl and sprinkle with the curry powder. Toss carefully and leave to marinate for 10 minutes.

Heat the oil to 375°C/190°F.

Deep fry the potatoes for 3–4 minutes. Drain on kitchen paper, season with salt and pepper and serve immediately.

Frizzled Leeks

Method
Slice the leek into very thin julienne strips about 6 cm in length. Season the flour with plenty of salt and pepper. Toss the leek strips in the seasoned flour. Deep fry the leeks in vegetable oil at 140°C/275°F gas mark 2 until golden brown.

Drain on kitchen paper and season lightly with more salt. Serve immediately or allow to cool and store in an airtight container. Reheat in a warm oven before serving.

Serves 4 as a garnish
1 leek, white part only
50 g plain flour
salt and freshly ground black pepper
vegetable oil

Roasted Peppers

Method

Preheat grill until very hot.

Cut the peppers in half and remove the seeds, stalk and inner membrane. Sprinkle a baking tray or roasting tin with sea salt and olive oil. Place the peppers skin side up on the tray and drizzle with some more olive oil. Place under the grill and after a few minutes the skin will start to char and blister. When the skins are black, place the peppers in a bowl. Cover with cling film and allow to cool. The skins will peel off easily.

4 peppers
sea salt
olive oil

Deep-fried Herbs and Vegetables

Our deep-fried garnishes add the finishing touch to a beautifully presented dish. They also provide a different texture.

Method

Use vegetable oil to cook the following.

Basil: Place basil leaves between two conical sieves or ladles so as to keep a flat shape and fry until crisp. Drain on kitchen paper and season lightly with salt.

Beetroot: Peel and slice as thinly as possible. Blanch in boiling water for 10 seconds. Drain and dry completely before frying until crisp. Drain on kitchen paper and season with salt.

Carrots: Peel and slice into very fine julienne strips and fry until crisp. Drain on kitchen paper and season with salt.

Celeriac Chips: Peel and slice as thinly as possible. Fry until crisp. Drain on kitchen paper and season lightly with salt.

Leeks: Using the white part only, slice into very fine julienne strips and fry until crisp. Drain on kitchen paper and season with salt.

Spinach: Finely slice, and fry until crisp (about 20–30 seconds). Drain on kitchen paper and season with salt.

Bread, olives and tapenade

DESSERTS

Banana and Coconut Soufflé

All the flavours of the Caribbean come together in this soufflé which is light in texture, but rich in taste.

The key to making a good soufflé is to have everything at hand, and working quickly. Most of the preparation can be done in advance. Make the crème patissière the night before and mix with the coconut, chocolate and banana. This leaves the egg whites to be whisked and folded in, and the soufflé to be baked. Use one large soufflé dish or 4–5 individual ones.

Method

Lightly grease the soufflé dish with butter and dust with cocoa powder. Tip out any excess. Melt the chocolate. Mix the melted chocolate, mashed banana and creamed coconut together. Add to the crème pâtissière and mix well. Chill until ready to use.

Preheat the oven to 200°C/400°F/gas mark 6.

Whisk the egg whites to soft peaks. Gradually add the sugar and continue to whisk until the whites form medium peaks. Fold the egg whites into the crème patissière. Immediately transfer to the prepared soufflé dish, filling it three-quarters full. Bake for 15–20 minutes. The soufflé should still be slightly soft in the middle.

To serve
Dust lightly with icing sugar and serve immediately.

Serves 4–5
butter for greasing
cocoa powder for dusting
50 g dark chocolate, chopped
1 banana, mashed
2 tablespoons creamed coconut
1 recipe crème patissière (see below)
4 egg whites
75 g sugar
icing sugar for dusting

Crème Patissière

Method

Bring the milk and the vanilla pod to the boil in a medium sized saucepan. Remove from the heat and allow to infuse for 10–15 minutes. Whisk the egg yolks and sugar together until pale and thickened, then whisk in the flour. Remove the vanilla pod from the milk and add the milk to the egg yolk mixture. Whisk, then strain into a clean saucepan.

Bring to the boil, whisking continuously. Reduce the heat and simmer for 2 minutes. Transfer to a bowl and allow to cool. To help prevent a skin forming, rub the surface of the crème with the butter. Once fully cooled, cover and chill until ready to use. It will keep overnight in the refrigerator.

Serves 4–5
250 ml milk
1 vanilla pod
3 egg yolks
60 g caster sugar
20 g flour

Chèvre Cheesecake with Praline Chocolate and Poached Mandarins

The tarragon cuts through the cheese of this very rich dessert.

Method

Start by making the base. Melt the chocolate in a bain marie. Add the rice crispies, granola and pistachios. Mix well and pour into a 20 cm flan ring with a removable base. Smooth out the base and chill until the filling is ready.

Soak the gelatine leaves in some cold water until soft.

Meanwhile place the cream cheese, goats' cheese, lemon and orange zest in a food processor and process until well combined.

Whisk the eggs and sugar over a bain marie.

Remove the gelatine from the water and gently squeeze dry. Melt in a saucepan over a very gentle heat. Do not stir. When the gelatine has turned to liquid, add it to the egg and sugar mix. Remove from the bain marie and continue to stir, adding the tarragon, lemon and orange juice.

Gradually pour the egg mixture into the cheese mixture, and process until all the egg and sugar mixture is well combined. As the mixture starts to cool, the gelatine should start to work and the mixture gradually thickens. If this is not happening, cool the filling over an ice bath and continue stirring. The mixture has to be cool before filling the flan ring.

Pour into the flan ring and chill until ready to serve.

To serve

Serve with the Poached Mandarins and sprigs of mint.

Serves 6–8

200 g praline/good quality milk chocolate
50 g rice crispies
50 g granola cereal
30 g pistachio nuts, toasted
2 gelatine leaves
250 g cream cheese
250 g goats' cheese
zest of 1 lemon
zest of 1 orange
6 eggs
170 g sugar
4 tablespoons tarragon, finely chopped
juice of 1 lemon
juice of 1 orange
1 recipe poached mandarins (see page 134)
6–8 sprigs mint

Chèvre Cheesecake with Praline Chocolate and Poached Mandarins

Warm Chocolate Fondants with Chocolate Sauce and Pistachio Ice Cream

Wickedly rich, but worth savouring every bite.

The fondants can be made well in advance, as they need to rest for at least 3 hours before baking. If you have an extra serving, it is always a good idea to use it as a 'tester' after cooking. Plate the tester first, before the others, to see how it has cooked. The mixture should still be soft in the centre, but able to hold its own shape. If it collapses too easily, simply cook the remaining fondants for a few more minutes.

Method
Preheat the oven to 190°C/375°F/gas mark 5.

Grease 6 dariole moulds with the butter and dust with cocoa powder. Tip out any excess powder.

Break the 150 g ungrated chocolate into pieces and melt in a bain marie. Gradually whisk in the butter and set aside. Whisk together the egg yolks and half the sugar. Mix with the chocolate and butter mixture.

In a separate bowl, whisk the egg whites with a teaspoon of sugar until stiff. Gradually add the remaining sugar and continue whisking until the mixture becomes shiny. Fold the egg whites into the chocolate mixture, along with the grated chocolate. Fill the dariole moulds two-thirds full of the fondant mixture, gently tapping to remove any trapped air bubbles. Cover with clingfilm and chill for at least 3–5 hours. Lightly press down the fondant mixture and bake for 6–8 minutes. Invert a dariole mould on to each plate and leave for a minute. Lightly tap and remove the mould.

To serve
Drizzle with chocolate sauce and serve immediately with scoops of Pistachio Ice Cream.

Serves 4–6
butter for greasing
cocoa powder for dusting
200 g dark chocolate, 50 g of which should be grated
75 g butter
3 eggs, separated
100 g sugar
1 recipe chocolate sauce (see page 138)
1 recipe pistachio ice cream (see page 150)

Warm Chocolate Fondants with Chocolate Sauce and Pistachio Ice Cream

Chocolate Sauce

This rich sauce is delicious with most ice creams and chocolate desserts.

Method

Melt the chocolate in a bain marie, stirring occasionally with a wooden spoon.

Bring the milk, cream and sugar to the boil in a medium saucepan, lightly whisking all the time. Remove from the heat and mix with the melted chocolate. Transfer to a clean saucepan and bring to the boil. Remove from the heat and whisk in the butter.

Allow to cool and chill until ready to use. The sauce may set slightly, but will become runny again once left at room temperature for half an hour. The sauce will keep overnight in the fridge.

Serves 4

200 g dark chocolate
150 ml milk
30 ml cream
30 g caster sugar
30 g butter, diced

Bitter Chocolate Tart

Rich and glossy, this tart has a beautifully silky texture.

The method for making the chocolate mixture is very simple. We think the key to its silky texture lies in the way it is cooked. It is never subjected to a blast of heat, only to moderate heat and is then left to cool in the oven for an hour to set.

Method

Preheat the oven to 180°C/350°F/gas mark 4.

Roll out the pastry to line a 30 cm flan rig with a removable base. Chill for 30 minutes. Line the pastry with greaseproof paper and fill with rice or dried beans.

Bake for approximately 10 minutes. Carefully remove the beans and greaseproof paper and return the pastry to the oven for a further five minutes, or until it's a pale golden colour and has quite a dry feel. Set aside until the filling is ready.

Place the cream and milk in a medium-sized saucepan and bring to the boil. Break the chocolate into small pieces and place in a large bowl. As soon as the cream mixture comes to the boil, carefully pour onto the chocolate and stir—the chocolate will start to melt. Keep stirring or whisking until all the chocolate has melted.

Fold in the eggs and pour into the prepared pastry case.

Place the tart in the oven and then turn the oven off. Leave the tart for 1¼ hours, by which time it should start to set. Remove from the oven and allow to cool to room temperature before serving.

You can refrigerate the tart until ready to serve, but bring it back to room temperature before serving.

To serve

Serve on its own or with Cappuccino Ice Cream (see page 149).

Serves 6–8
½ recipe sweet pastry (see page 142)
350 ml cream
200 ml milk
500g good quality dark chocolate
3 eggs beaten

Lemon Tart with Basil and Lemon Sorbet and Peppered Blackberry Coulis

This delicious dessert goes beautifully with the peppered blackberry coulis and the sharp but refreshing sorbet.

Make individual tarts or one large tart. Slice with a hot knife when serving.

Method

Preheat the oven to 180°C/350°F/gas mark 4.

Roll out the pastry as thinly as possible to line a 25 cm flan ring with a removable base. Line the pastry with greaseproof paper and fill with rice or dried beans. Chill for 30 minutes.

Bake blind for 10 minutes. Carefully remove the beans and greaseproof paper. Sprinkle the pastry case with the demerara sugar and return to the oven for a further five minutes or until it is a pale golden colour and has quite a dry feel.

Heat together the butter and crème fraîche in a bain marie. Stir continuously until the mixture is smooth and warm. Set aside.

In a separate bowl, whisk the egg and yolks. Place this bowl in the bain marie and continue whisking while adding the crème fraîche mixture. When this is well combined, add the lemon juice. Mix well and then strain through a fine sieve into a clean bowl. Place the bowl in the bain marie. Add the sugar and lemon rind and continue to whisk until the mixture is quite frothy on the surface. At this stage, stop whisking and stir gently with a wooden spoon for about 5 minutes until the foam starts to disappear.

Pour the filling into the tart or individual tarts. Bake for approximately 20 minutes (10–15 minutes for the individual ones) until the filling is just starting to set. Turn the oven off and allow to set in the oven for a further 10–20 minutes. Allow the tart to cool fully and chill for an hour before serving.

To serve

Garnish with citrus confit and serve with the chilled coulis and scoops of sorbet.

Serves 6–8

½ recipe sweet pastry (see page 142)
2 teaspoons demerara sugar
30 g unsalted butter
200 g crème fraîche
5 eggs
4 egg yolks
juice of 8 lemons
200 g sugar
rind of 5 lemons
1 recipe peppered blackberry coulis (see page 152)
2 recipes basil and lemon sorbet (see page 151)
1 recipe citrus confit (see page 142)

Lemon Tart with Basil and Lemon Sorbet and Peppered Blackberry Coulis

Sweet Pastry

This sweet pastry is similar to those Alain Ducasse uses in Monte Carlo. Instead of using water to bind the pastry, cream is added which gives the pastry a creamy, biscuity texture. It can be quite tricky to work with, and to line a flan ring. The important thing is to chill the pastry sufficiently before working and to work somewhere cool when rolling it out. You may feel that you are using excessive amounts of flour to help prevent the pastry from sticking when rolling it, but don't worry—it is so rich it can absorb the extra flour easily.

The more you practise the more proficient you will become at rolling and lining pastry. Remember, pastry chefs train for years to learn their trade and perfect their skills.

110 g icing sugar
120 g butter
1 egg and 1 egg yolk, beaten together
2 tablespoons cream
300 g flour

Method
This is easiest made in the food processor. Cream together the sugar and butter, add the eggs and cream and process on the pulse mode.

Add the flour and process until the mixture comes together. Wrap in cling film and chill for at least 30 minutes. The pastry will keep overnight in the fridge.

When you cream the eggs and sugar, try not to overprocess, because when the eggs and cream are added the mixture can look as if it has split. But as soon as you mix in the flour it returns to normal.

Citrus Confit

Use one fruit or a combination of all three.

Serves 4
zest of 4 oranges, limes or lemons, or a combination
100 ml stock syrup (see page 151)

Method
Blanch the zest in boiling water for about 10 seconds. Immediately drain and refresh in cold running water. Drain thoroughly, place in a small saucepan with the stock syrup and bring to the boil. Reduce the heat and simmer for about 20 minutes. Cool fully and store in the syrup, chilled, for up to 3 days. Drain thoroughly before serving.

Rhubarb Tart

The rosemary cooked with the rhubarb cuts through the sweet and creamy filling in a really interesting combination of flavours.

The sauté rhubarb is so delicious it is good enough to serve on its own.

Method

Preheat the oven to 200°C/400°F/gas mark 6.

Roll out the pastry to line a 30 cm flan ring with a removable base. Line the pastry with greaseproof paper and fill with rice or dried beans. Bake for approximately 10 minutes. Carefully remove the beans or rice and greaseproof paper and return the pastry to the oven for a further five minutes, or until it's a pale golden colour and has quite a dry feel. Set aside until the filling is ready.

Melt the butter in a large saucepan and add the rhubarb. Cook over a medium heat for 10 minutes. The rhubarb should start to break down. Add the sugar, maple syrup, rosemary and vanilla pod. Continue to cook gently until the rhubarb is very soft. Taste and add more sugar, syrup or a squeeze of lemon juice if you feel that it is too sweet. The mixture will be quite runny, but will thicken up as it cools. Set aside until completely cool before filling the tart.

To make the crumble topping, simply place the flour, butter and sugar in a food processor and process on the pulse button until the mixture resembles breadcrumbs. Wrap in clingfilm and chill until required.

Preheat the oven to 180°C/350°F/ gas mark 4.

Pour the filling into the tart and then sprinkle the crumble topping over the filling. Bake for 25 minutes until the crumble mixture has turned a light brown. Watch that the edges of the sweet pastry don't start to burn. If they do, wrap them in some tin foil. Sprinkle the top with the pistachios. Allow to cool for five minutes before slicing.

To serve

Serve with Pistachio Ice Cream (see page 150).

Serves 4

½ recipe sweet pastry (see page 142)
100 g butter
800 g rhubarb, roughly chopped
90 g demerera sugar
6 tablespoons maple syrup
2 sprigs rosemary
1 vanilla pod
juice of ½ lemon

Crumble topping
100g plain flour
50g butter, chilled
50 g demerara sugar
50 g pistachios, toasted and finely chopped

Peach Tarte Tatin

The delicious pastry combined with the buttery caramel flavour of the fruit make this a favourite dessert.

Tarte Tatin is the name given to the 'upside down tart' made famous by the Tatin sisters and served at Maxim's in Paris. It can also be made with pears and apples. Make sure you cook the tarte in a frying pan that has a metal handle as the pan has to be transferred to the oven.

Method
Preheat the oven 190°C/375°F/gas mark 5.

Sift together the flour and rice into a large bowl. Rub in the butter until the mixture resembles breadcrumbs and then add the eggs to bind. Wrap in clingfilm and chill for at least 30 minutes.

Peel and stone the peaches. Cut into quarters or eighths. Melt the butter in a large ovenproof frying pan, and then add the sugar. Arrange the peaches rounded side down in the pan, starting at the outside and working into the middle of the pan.

Turn the heat up and allow the butter and sugar to caramelise. This process should take at least 7 minutes, and by then the caramel should have started to darken and you should be able to smell the caramel. You will need to turn the pan around from time to time to ensure that the peaches caramelise evenly. Sprinkle the lemon rind, star anise and cinnamon onto the peaches and remove from the heat.

Roll the pastry to ¾ cm thick and place on top of the peaches. Trim away any excess pastry and lightly press down. Bake in the oven for 25–30 minutes or until the pastry is golden brown. Remove from the oven and cool for ten minutes before inverting onto a plate and serving.

To serve
Serve warm with some Caramel Ice Cream (see page 149).

Serves 4–6

Pastry
175 g flour
50 g ground rice
140 g butter
50 g caster sugar
1 egg, beaten

Topping
1 kg peaches
125 g butter
125 g granulated sugar
rind of 1 lemon
½ teaspoon star anise
½ teaspoon cinnamon

Creamed Rice Pudding with Baked Spiced Plums and Crème Chantilly

Like a sweet vanilla risotto, this pudding served with plums flavoured with spice and mango is comfort food taken to the limit!

Be warned—your eyes will definitely be bigger than your stomach here.

Method

Bring the milk and cream to the boil in a large saucepan, along with the vanilla seeds, sugar and butter.

Add the rice, bring the mixture back to the boil and then reduce the heat and simmer for 25–30 minutes. Allow to cool.

When you have cooked the rice, the mixture will probably look quite runny but it does thicken considerably as it cools down. You can serve the pudding at this stage or allow to cool fully and reheat as required with the extra milk and cream.

When ready to serve, heat the extra milk and cream in a small saucepan adding enough to the pudding to achieve the desired consistency and heat through.

To serve

Serve topped with Baked Spiced Plums and Crème Chantilly drizzled around the bowl.

Serves 4
40 ml milk
400 ml cream
1 vanilla pod, split and seeds scraped out
50 g sugar
30 g butter
75 g short/round grain pudding rice
extra 100 ml milk (optional)
extra 100 ml cream (optional)
1 recipe baked spiced plums (see page 146)
1 recipe crème chantilly (see page 146)

Baked Spiced Plums

These are also a wonderful accompaniment to ice cream or crème fraîche. Peaches cooked in the same way are also delicious.

Serves 4
4–6 plums
1 recipe mango coulis (see page 152)
½ teaspoon star anise
½ teaspoon cinnamon
30 g butter
2 tablespoons sugar

Method
Preheat the oven to 190°C/375°F/gas mark 5.

Cut the plums in half and remove the stones. Place the plums skin side down in an ovenproof dish and drizzle with mango coulis. Sprinkle the remaining ingredients on top and bake for 10 minutes.

Remove from the oven and baste with the cooking juices. Allow to cool until ready to serve.

Preheat the grill to a high setting. Grill the plums until they have warmed through and the edges have started to caramelise. Serve as required.

Crème Chantilly

Serve with fruit desserts.

Serves 4
1 vanilla pod
200 ml cream
25 g icing sugar

Method
Split the vanilla pod, and scrape out one-third of the seeds into a bowl with the cream and icing sugar. Whisk the cream until light and frothy. Chill until ready to serve.

Wine Suggestion for Desserts

Good dessert wines are a thing unto themselves, long-lived, intense, balanced and not at all cloyingly sweet. Bad dessert wines are merely sweet, lacking in structure and balance. It is wise to spend the money—in effect make a dessert of the wine itself.

Good Sauternes has a full-flavoured lusciousness that will go with most desserts, but unfortunately it costs a lot of money to move up to Yquem. Barsac can also be superb and a touch drier than Sauternes. Excellent late-harvest sweet wines are emerging in the New World. Some Greek sweet wines, including Maphrodaphne, can be superb. The famous Hungarian Tokaji is being revived.

Port, sweet sherry and Madeira are effective with most desserts. You can also try sweet Italian or southern French wines such as Marsala or Banyuls with rich puddings or chocolate dishes.

Sweet sparkling wine also works well with fruity desserts. French Monbazillac is perfect with crème brûlée.

One of the most intense sweet wine experiences comes from good ice wine, in German eiswein. Canada is producing wonderfully intense ice wine, which is available in North America and Asia, but is difficult to find in Europe.

And surprisingly, if you find yourself drinking a fine old claret with the cheese course, which traditionally comes before dessert, you may find it also works quite well with a sweet course.

Ice Creams

In Peacock Alley ice creams and sorbets are made fresh every day, using an electric ice cream machine. This is the best and most convenient way of making ice cream, as the mixture is simultaneously churned and frozen, giving a very smooth and creamy texture. This continuous churning slows down the formation of ice crystals which can give an 'icy' texture. The ice cream recipes are basically a crème anglaise base with additional flavourings.

Whether you use an ice cream machine or a freezer, add the additional ingredients, e.g. chopped chocolate, towards the end of freezing when the ice cream has nearly set. If you are not using a machine, remove the ice cream or sorbet from the container in the freezer several times and blend it in a food processor to help break up the formation of ice crystals. Use the pulse button as overprocessing could cause curdling.

Crème Anglaise

Method

Heat together the milk, cream and vanilla pod. Bring to the boil and allow to infuse for 10 minutes.

Whisk the sugar and egg yolks until pale and creamy, and 'to the ribbon'. Bring the milk mixture to the boil again and gradually pour onto the whisked eggs. Return the mixture to the saucepan and cook over a very gentle heat, until the mixture coats the back of a wooden spoon. This should take 2–3 minutes. Strain the mixture and cool in an ice bath. It will keep in the fridge for 24 hours.

600 ml milk
300 ml cream
1 vanilla pod (optional)
250 g caster sugar
8 egg yolks

[148]

Cappuccino Ice Cream

Method

Make the coffee using good quality coffee—we usually use Illy espresso. Reduce the coffee by half in a small saucepan. Mix well with the crème anglaise and freeze until almost set.

Add the chocolate and continue to churn in the ice cream machine or use the pulse button of a food-processor until well-mixed. Freeze until ready to serve.

Serves 4–6
200 ml strong black coffee
1 recipe crème anglaise, (see page 148) made without the vanilla pod
100 g dark chocolate, finely chopped

Caramel Ice Cream

Method

Bring the milk, cream and vanilla pod to the boil and allow to infuse. Remove the vanilla pod. Make a dry caramel with the granulated sugar. Heat the sugar gently in a small saucepan, allowing it to dissolve and then increase the heat so that the sugar turns a brown caramel colour. Remove from the heat and very carefully add the hot cream mixture. Beware of the caramel spitting and spluttering!

Whisk the sugar and egg yolks until pale and creamy, and 'to the ribbon'. Pour the caramel and cream mixture on to the egg yolk mixture. Return the mixture to the saucepan and cook over a very gentle heat, until the mixture coats the back of a wooden spoon. This should take 2–3 minutes. Strain the mixture. Freeze until ready to serve.

Note: When making a dry caramel it is very important not to stir the sugar or it will crystallise. If the sugar starts to crystallise around the sides of the pan, brush the sides down with a pastry brush dipped in cold water.

Serves 4–6
600 ml milk
300 ml cream
1 vanilla pod (optional)
150 g granulated sugar
250 g caster sugar
8 egg yolks

Cinnamon and Crème Fraîche Ice Cream

The crème fraîche gives extra body to this ice cream.

Method

Proceed exactly as for the crème anglaise recipe, replacing the vanilla pod with the cinnamon stick. Freeze in the ice cream machine or plastic container until almost set.

Add the crème fraîche and the ground cinnamon and continue to churn in the ice cream machine or blend in the food processor until well mixed. Freeze until ready to serve.

Serves 4–6
1 recipe crème anglaise (see page 148), made without the vanilla pod
1 cinnamon stick
70 g crème fraîche
1 teaspoon ground cinnamon

Pistachio Ice Cream

Method

Preheat the oven to 200°C/400°F/gas mark 6.

Mix the pistachio paste with the crème anglaise and freeze until almost set. Place the pistachios on a baking tray lined with greaseproof paper, lightly sprinkle with the icing sugar, and cook in the oven for approximately 5 minutes or until lightly toasted.

Remove from the oven and allow to cool before grinding in a food processor. Add the pistachios to the ice cream and continue to churn in the ice cream machine or blend in the food processor until well mixed. Freeze until ready to serve.

Serves 4–6

3 tablespoons pistachio paste, (available in specialist shops)
1 recipe crème anglaise (see page 148), made without the vanilla pods
50 g pistachio nuts, skinned
1 tablespoon icing sugar

Thyme Ice Cream

Method

Follow the crème anglaise recipe, but replace the vanilla pod with the thyme. Freeze in an ice cream machine or a plastic container.

Serves 4–6

1 recipe crème anglaise, made without the vanilla pod (see page 148)
5 sprigs thyme

Chèvre Ice Cream

Method

Proceed as for the crème anglaise recipe up to the stage of heatng the custard. Add the goats' cheese and mix well. Continue to follow the crème anglaise recipe and freeze in the ice cream machine or plastic container until ready to serve.

Serves 4–6

1 recipe crème anglaise (see page 148)
200 g goats' cheese

Basil and Lemon Sorbet

The basil takes on a sweet and fragrant flavour in this sorbet, which is deliciously refreshing at the end of a meal, but is also good to serve between courses to refresh the palate.

Using stock syrup for the base, follow the same principle when making sorbets as when making ice cream (see page 148), adding the whisked egg whites just before the sorbet has set.

Method

Follow the recipe for stock syrup but do not use the cinnamon stick. Add the lemon juice to the syrup as it's cooling and then strain. Freeze in an ice cream machine or plastic container until almost set. Add the basil and egg whites and continue to churn in the ice cream machine until well mixed or mix well in the container. Freeze until ready to serve.

Serves 4–6
3 recipes stock syrup (see below)
juice of 8–10 lemons
50 g basil leaves, finely sliced
2 egg whites

Stock Syrup

Method

Place the sugar, water and glucose in a small saucepan and heat gently until the sugar has dissolved.

Tip: before dipping into the glucose, warm the spoon in hot water: the glucose will come away from the spoon more easily when adding it to the saucepan.

Add the lemon, orange and cinnamon stick and bring to the boil. Reduce the heat and simmer for 5 minutes. Allow to cool slightly and strain. Cool fully and then chill, covered, until ready to use. The stock syrup will keep for a week in the refrigerator.

150g caster sugar
250 ml water
1 teaspoon glucose
½ lemon
½ orange
1 cinnamon stick (optional)

[151]

Coulis

Coulis are delicious served with ice creams and desserts such as rice pudding and they make excellent garnishes for dessert plates. In the strict sense they are liquid purées made from vegetables, shellfish or fruit and should be of a thin consistency to pour easily. They should always be strained and should not be too watery. During the 1980s, nouvelle cuisine brought a surge in the use of coulis but the term was generalised to describe most fruit and vegetable sauces regardless of their consistency. They have since become a little unfashionable but you should ignore food trends!

Mango Coulis

Remove the flesh from the mango and place in a food processor or blender along with the stock syrup and lemon juice. Purée until smooth. Pass through a fine sieve and chill until ready to serve.

Serves 4–6
4–5 mangoes
½ recipe of stock syrup (see page 151)
juice of 1 lemon

Pear Coulis

Place the ingredients in a food processor or blender and purée until smooth. Pass through a fine sieve and chill until ready to serve.

Serves 4–6
2 pears, peeled, cored and chopped
½ recipe of stock syrup (see page 151)

Peppered Blackberry Coulis

Blend the blackberries, stock syrup and lemon juice in a food processor until smooth. Pass through a sieve and then stir in the black pepper. Chill until ready to serve.

Serves 4–6
100 g blackberries
½ recipe of stock syrup (see page 151)
juice of 1 lemon
½ teaspoon freshly ground black pepper

PETITS FOURS

Baileys Irish Cream Truffles

These truffles are velvety smooth without being overpoweringly rich.

Method

Whisk the sugar and eggs until pale. Place over a bain marie and stir until the mixture coats the back of a spoon. Set aside.

Bring the cream to the boil and carefully pour onto the chocolate. Stir until the chocolate has melted and then mix with the egg mixture. Add the Baileys and cool. When the mixture is cool, place it in a freezer to set for at least 30 minutes.

When set, roll teaspoonfuls of the truffle mixture into ball shapes, and lightly coat with cocoa powder. Refrigerate or freeze until required. The truffles will keep for 2–3 days in the refrigerator and up to 1 week frozen.

Sheridan's Truffles

Follow the recipe above substituting 2 tablespoons of Sheridan's for the Baileys.

Pistachio Truffles

Follow the recipe above but do not add any alcohol. Toast 100 g pistachio nuts and finely chop. Roll the truffles in the chopped nuts instead of the cocoa powder. These truffles are velvety smooth without being overpoweringly rich.

Yields 25–30 truffles

50 g caster sugar
2 egg yolks
75 ml cream
125 g good quality dark chocolate, grated
2 tablespoons of Baileys Irish Cream
cocoa powder for dusting

Lemon Meringue Tartlets

These are cooked at a very intense heat for only 3 minutes. If your oven doesn't go that high, just bake them for a little longer. Alternatively you can blast them with a blow torch!

Method

Preheat the oven to 180°C/350°F/gas mark 4.

Roll the pastry as thinly as possible and make sure there are no holes. Line 30 small tartlet tins. Cover the pastry with greaseproof paper and fill the tartlet tins with beans or rice. Bake for 6–7 minutes, remove the paper and beans and bake for a further 1–2 minutes until golden brown. Cool on a wire rack. Store in an airtight container until ready to use.

Boil the lemon juice and butter in a small saucepan. Whisk the eggs and sugar together until creamy and add the hot butter mixture. Using a clean medium-sized saucepan, cook the custard over a gentle heat, stirring constantly, until it coats the back of a spoon. Do not allow it to boil or it will curdle.

Transfer to a clean bowl and allow to cool—the custard will continue to thicken. Cover with clingfilm and chill until ready to use.

Whisk the egg whites until they form stiff peaks. Gradually whisk in the sugar, until the mixture is stiff and shiny.

Preheat the oven to 250°C/500°F/gas mark 10.

Using a piping bag with a 1 cm nozzle, pipe a small amount of custard into each tartlet. Using a 1 cm star-shaped nozzle, pipe some meringue on top. Bake for approximately 3 minutes or until the meringue is cooked. Allow to cool before serving.

Makes 30
100 g sweet pastry (see page 142)

Lemon custard filling
50 ml lemon juice
25 g unsalted butter
1½ eggs
60 g caster sugar

Meringue
2 egg whites
55 g sugar

Honey Wafers

Serve these with any creamy dessert such as crème brûlée, ice cream or parfaits.

Method
Preheat the oven to 180°C/350°F/gas mark 4.

Cream the butter and sugar together in a mixing bowl until light and fluffy, then gradually add the honey. Sift together the flour, salt and cinnamon and fold into the butter mixture.

Transfer the mixture into a piping bag with a 1 cm round nozzle and cover a baking tray with greaseproof paper. Pipe 4 cm lengths of the mixture on to the paper, leaving 4 cm spaces in between, as the wafers will spread while cooking. Bake in the oven for 5–7 minutes or until the edges of the wafers start to turn golden brown. Transfer to a wire rack to cool and serve as required. Store in an airtight container for up to a day.

Makes 15–20
30 g butter
35 g icing sugar
60 g honey
40 g flour
pinch of salt
pinch of cinnamon

Madeleines

Method
Preheat the oven to 180°C/350°F/gas mark 4.

In a food processor, mix together the flour, sugar and baking powder. Leave the motor running. Add the egg and egg yolk and pour in the clarified butter. When the mixture is smooth, chill for at least two hours.

Transfer the mixture into a piping bag with a 1 cm round nozzle. Pipe the mixture into greased madeleine moulds or into desired shapes on a baking tray lined with greaseproof paper. Bake for about 12 minutes until a pale golden colour. Serve immediately or allow to cool and store in an airtight container for up a day.

Makes 30–40
50 g flour
50 g sugar
1 teaspoon baking powder
1 egg
1 egg yolk
60 g clarified unsalted butter, melted (see page 173)

Brandy Snaps with Toasted Sesame Seeds

Brandy snaps are very pliable when they're warm and can be made into cigar or basket shapes to suit your requirements.

Method

Preheat the oven to 170°C/325°F/gas mark 3. Melt together the butter, sugar and golden syrup, then remove from the heat. Sift the flour and ginger together and add to the butter mixture. Mix well and add the lemon juice. Set aside until cool enough to handle.

Line two large baking trays with greaseproof paper and place teaspoon-size balls on to the baking trays, leaving plenty of room between them, as they will spread during cooking. Lightly pat the brandy snaps flat and sprinkle with the sesame seeds. Bake until golden brown, approximately 4–5 minutes.

Remove from the baking trays and shape into cigars around greased wooden spoon handles or baskets around the end of a greased rolling pin. Do this while the snaps are still warm, as they become brittle when cold. If the brandy snaps are cooling too quickly, place them back in the oven briefly to warm them through and reshape. Continue baking and shaping until all the mixture is used. Allow to cool fully and serve or store in an airtight container for up to three days.

Makes about 20
55 g unsalted butter
55 g sugar
3 tablespoons golden syrup
55 g flour
pinch of ground ginger
juice of 1 lemon
30 g sesame seeds, lightly toasted

Coconut Tuiles

Method

Preheat the oven to 180°C/350°F/gas mark 4.

Cream the butter and sugar together. Sift the flour, add to the creamed butter and sugar and mix well. Lightly whisk the egg whites until soft peaks form and fold into the creamed butter mixture. Line two baking trays with greaseproof paper and spoon small balls of the mixture on to the paper and pat down. Leave a lot of room between, as the mixture will spread during cooking. Sprinkle with the coconut and bake for 4–5 minutes until golden brown. Remove from the baking tray and shape around the end of a greased rolling pin to form a basket shape. Try to do this quickly, as the tuiles become brittle once they've cooked. Continue baking and shaping until you've used up all the mixture. Allow to cool fully and serve, or keep in an airtight container for up to three days.

Makes 20–25
100 g butter
100 g icing sugar
75 g flour
4 egg whites
50 g desiccated coconut, lightly toasted

BREAD, STOCK, FLAVOURED OILS AND VINAIGRETTES

Breads and Rolls

Treacle Bread

This is a rich and wholesome bread—moist and slightly sweet on the inside and crisp on the outside. It is best eaten while still warm from the oven with some unsalted butter or some good Irish cheese.

Method
Preheat the oven to 160°C/325°F/gas mark 3.

Sieve the flours, bread soda and salt into a large mixing bowl. Add any bran left in the sieve to the flours in the bowl. Add the oatmeal, sugar and bran and mix well.

In a small saucepan, gently heat together the treacle and butter. When the butter has melted, gradually add the buttermilk and stir until well blended.

Add to the mixture in the bowl and mix well—the result will be a very wet and sticky dough. Pour into 2 lightly greased 450 g loaf tins and bake for 1–1½ hours.

After an hour, if the loaves are firm enough, or longer if not sufficiently cooked, remove them from the tins and place them on a baking tray or wire rack, and continue baking for about half an hour. This helps develop a crisp crust all over. The bread is ready if it sounds a little hollow when tapped underneath. This bread tastes better if left for 24 hours. If you are going to keep it overnight, do not slice until ready to serve.

Makes 2 loaves
500 g wholemeal flour
125 g strong white flour
2 teaspoons bread soda
2 teaspoons salt
65 g pinhead oatmeal
1 tablespoon demerara sugar
65 g wheat bran
80 ml treacle
50 g butter
1 litre buttermilk

Guinness Bread

Method

Preheat the oven to 160°C/325°F/gas mark 3.

Sieve the flours, bread soda and salt into a large mixing bowl. Add any bran that is left in the sieve to the flours in the bowl. Add the oatmeal, sugar and bran and mix well.

In a small saucepan, gently heat together the treacle and butter. When the butter has melted, add the Guinness and the milk. Stir well.

Combine the flours and the liquid mixtures. The resulting dough will be quite wet. Pour into a lightly greased 450 g loaf tin, and bake for 1–1½ hours.

After an hour, providing the loaf is firm enough, remove it from the tin and place it directly on a rack in the oven. This will ensure an even crust. However, watch that the bread doesn't brown too quickly due to the high sugar content. If this is happening, cover the loaf with tin foil.

The loaf should not feel dense and when cooked should sound a little hollow when tapped underneath.

Allow to cool slightly before slicing. The bread tastes even better if left for 24 hours. If you are going to keep it overnight, do not slice until you are ready to serve.

Makes 1 loaf

250 g wholemeal flour
60 g strong white flour
1 teaspoon bread soda
1 teaspoon salt
30 g pinhead oatmeal
1 teaspoon demerara sugar
30 g wheat bran
4 tablespoons treacle
30 g butter
100 ml Guinness
200 ml milk

Apricot and Curry Bread with Polenta

This is a great combination of spicy and sweet flavours. It goes especially well with the Crabmeat and Beetroot Salad (see page 43) as it enhances the curried crème fraîche and brings out the sweetness in the beetroot.

Method

Sift together the flour, salt and curry powder into a large mixing bowl. Make a well in the centre.

Cream together the yeast, sugar and a small amount of the water. Pour into the well together with the olive oil and enough of the remaining water to make a soft dough. Mix and then knead until smooth and elastic.

Place the dough into a clean mixing bowl and cover with lightly greased clingfilm. Leave to rise at room temperature until doubled in size—this should take at least an hour.

Add the apricots and knead for 2 minutes. Divide the dough into 4 pieces. Roll and stretch into long baguette shapes. Sprinke ¼ of the polenta onto a clean work surface and roll each baguette in the polenta until evenly coated. Repeat this process with the remaining 3 baguettes and polenta. Place all 4 baguettes onto 2 lightly greased baking trays and leave to prove until doubled in size.

Preheat the oven to 200°C/400°F/gas mark 6.

Carefully glaze the loaves with the beaten egg and sprinkle with any remaining polenta. Bake for 15 minutes and then cool on a wire rack. The bread should feel quite light but if it feels dense, return to the oven for a further 5–10 minutes.

Makes 2 loaves
500 g strong white flour
2 teaspoons salt
30 g curry powder
15 g fresh yeast
1 teaspoon sugar
270 ml lukewarm water
40 ml olive oil
50 g dried apricots, finely chopped
100 g polenta
1 egg, beaten

Sundried Tomato Bread

You could also flavour this bread with herbs such as thyme or rosemary.

Method

In a food processor, mix together the flour and salt. Cream the yeast with the sugar and a few tablespoons of water.

Add the yeast and ¾ of the water to the flour and process. Add the tomato purée, tapenade/sundried tomatoes, basil and olive oil. The dough should come together and feel quite soft but not sticky. Add more water if necessary.

Turn the dough out onto a lightly floured surface and knead until smooth and elastic (this should take about ten minutes). Place the dough in a lightly greased bowl, cover with clingfilm and leave to rise for 1½–2 hours until doubled in size.

Knock back the dough and shape into a long baguette. Place the dough on a baking tray and leave to prove for about ¾–1 hour until doubled in size. Leave the dough covered with a damp tea towel.

Preheat the oven to 200°C/400°F/gas mark 6.

Lightly glaze the dough with some beaten egg. Bake for 15 minutes and then turn down the oven to 180°C/350°F/gas mark 4.

Bake for a further 25 minutes, or until the loaf sounds hollow when tapped underneath. Cool on a wire rack and use as required.

Makes 1 loaf

750 g flour
1 teaspoon salt
15 g fresh yeast
1 teaspoon sugar
2–300 ml warm water, approximately
4 tablespoons tomato purée
200 g sundried tomato tapenade (see page 69) or sundried tomatoes in olive oil, drained and finely chopped
1 tablespoon basil, finely chopped
4 tablespoons olive oil
1 egg, beaten

Focaccia

Focaccia is especially good when served with flavoured olive oils and tapenade, or used for sandwiches. Spraying it with water before baking and then once again after 15 minutes in the oven helps to give it a beautiful crust and golden colour.

Method

Mix together the flour, salt and pepper in a large bowl.

Cream the yeast with a small amount of the water and add to the flour with the rest of the water and 3 tablespoons of olive oil. Mix together until you have a very soft but not sticky dough. Add more water and flour if necessary. Turn out onto a clean work surface and knead for 10 minutes until smooth and elastic.

Lightly grease a large bowl with olive oil and place the dough in it. Turn the dough over onto each side so that it gets evenly coated with oil, cover with a damp tea towel and leave to rise for about 2 hours at room temperature until doubled in size.

Brush a roasting tin with olive oil. Add the basil, black olives, garlic and sundried tomatoes to the dough and knead for 1 minute. Transfer to the roasting tin and push the dough into the corners. Cover with a damp tea towel and leave to rise at room temperature for about1 hour or until doubled in size.

Preheat oven to 220°C/440°F/ gas mark 7.

Dimple the dough with your fingers, drizzle with the remaining olive oil and sprinkle with the sea salt. Spray with some water and bake for 15–20 minutes. Remove the bread from the oven and spray with more water and sprinkle the rosemary and thyme on top. Reduce the oven temperature to 220°F/400°C/gas mark 6. Bake for another 15–20 minutes or until golden brown. Cool on a wire rack and serve.

Makes 1 large loaf

500 g strong flour
2 teaspoons salt
1 teaspoon freshly ground black pepper
15 g yeast
220 ml water
5 tablespoons olive oil
extra olive oil for greasing bowl and roasting tin
2 tablespoons basil, finely chopped
2 tablespoons black olives, finely chopped
2 cloves garlic, peeled and finely chopped
2 tablespoons sundried tomatoes, finely chopped
2 tablespoons coarse sea salt
4 sprigs rosemary
4 sprigs thyme

Dill and Onion Rolls

These are best when served straight from the oven. They go especially well with the sundried tomato tapenade (see page 69).

Method

Preheat the oven to 220°C/425°F/gas mark 7.

Sift the flour and salt into a mixing bowl and make a well in the centre. Cream the yeast with the sugar and a little water. Add to the flour along with enough water to make quite a wet dough.

Bring the mixture together and turn out on to a lightly floured surface. Knead until the dough is no longer sticking to the work surface. You may have to sprinkle on some extra flour to help achieve this.

Place the dough in a clean bowl and cover with lightly greased clingfilm. Allow to rise at room temperature until doubled in size; this will take about 1½–2 hours.

Add the onion and dill and knead for a few minutes until they are well incorporated. Divide the mixture into small rolls and place them on a lightly greased baking tray. Leave to prove until doubled in size—about 30 minutes.

Glaze with the beaten egg and bake for 10–15 minutes. Cool slightly on a wire rack before serving.

Makes 25 small rolls

500 g strong white flour
2 teaspoons salt
15 g fresh yeast
1 teaspoon caster sugar
290 ml lukewarm water
1 tablespoon olive oil
1 red onion, peeled and finely chopped
1 tablespoon dill, finely chopped
1 egg, beaten

Stocks

Chicken Stock

We use chicken stock for most of our sauces, polentas and risottos.

Method

Place the chicken bones in a large saucepan and add the water. Bring to the boil. Skim any scum or impurities that rise to the surface. Once the stock has boiled, add the remaining ingredients.

Bring to the boil once more, reduce the heat and simmer gently for at least 4 hours. Skim the stock regularly. Cool slightly and then remove the bones or carcasses.

Strain through a fine sieve or preferably muslin. Discard the vegetables and bones. Reduce the stock by rapid boiling if it lacks flavour. Otherwise cool and then refrigerate or freeze.

Yields about 1 litre
2 kg raw chicken bones, carcasses or other joints
3 litres cold water
1 leek, roughly chopped
1 carrot, peeled and roughly chopped
1 onion, unpeeled, roughly chopped
1 sprig rosemary
salt and freshly ground black pepper

Beef or Veal Stock

A good meat stock contains a high level of gelatine, which comes from the bone and gives the stock more body.

Method

Preheat the oven to 200°C/400°F/gas mark 6.

Place the bones in a large roasting tin. Smear with 200 ml of the olive oil and season well. Roast in the oven for up to 2 hours until very well browned.

Heat the remaining olive oil in a very large saucepan and sauté the onion, shallots, carrots, celery and garlic until well browned. Add the red wine and simmer until reduced by half. Add the water, mix well, and add the bones and bouquet garni. Bring to the boil and simmer uncovered for at least 4 hours. Using a metal spoon, occasionally skim any fat or impurities from the surface. It may be necessary to add more water, as the bones must be kept covered.

When the stock is ready, remove the bones, strain the stock through a colander and then through muslin or a fine sieve. Transfer to a clean saucepan and reduce by at least half. Allow to cool and reheat or freeze as required.

Yields about 2 litres
2 kg veal or beef bones
125 ml olive oil
salt and freshly ground black pepper
1 large onion, unpeeled, roughly chopped
2 shallots, unpeeled, roughly chopped
2 large carrots, peeled and roughly chopped
2 celery sticks, roughly chopped
4 cloves of garlic, peeled and chopped
½ bottle red wine
8 litres cold water
1 bay leaf
1 sprig of thyme

Lamb Stock

Using a good chicken stock instead of water gives plenty of flavour. Avoid overseasoning as the stock is reduced a great deal to get a good flavour. If you add too much salt, you will end up with a salt and lamb stock.

Method

Preheat the oven to 200°C/400°F/gas mark 6.

Pour a tablespoon of olive oil into a large roasting tray. Add the bones and roast in the oven until well browned, which should take about 40 minutes. Turn the bones occasionally to ensure an even colour.

Meanwhile, heat the remaining olive oil in a large saucepan and sauté the shallots. Season with a small amount of salt and pepper. When the shallots have browned evenly, add the garlic, horseradish and tomato purée. Cook for a further 5 minutes and then add the herbs and stock or water. Bring to the boil, reduce the heat, and simmer for 3 hours.

Skim the stock regularly to remove any fat and impurities. When the stock is ready, remove the bones and pass the stock through a fine sieve or muslin three times. After straining reduce the stock to about half by rapid boiling.

Yields 500 ml

2 tablespoons olive oil
1 kg lamb bones
10 shallots, peeled and roughly chopped
salt and freshly ground black pepper
2 cloves garlic, peeled and crushed
1 tablespoon grated horseradish
1 tablespoon tomato purée
½ teaspoon tarragon, chopped
2 sprigs of rosemary
1½ litres chicken stock or water

Vegetable Stock

In Peacock Alley, we always have some vegetable stock at hand to use when cooking for vegetarians.

Think carefully about the end flavour that you want to achieve—too many carrots make the stock too sweet, and cabbage gives an overpowering taste. We use fennel and leeks as well as plenty of fresh herbs, but never use the stock pot as a dumping ground for any leftover vegetables. We treat the stock as a dish in its own right.

Method

Place all the ingredients except the herbs and water in a large saucepan and cook for 15 minutes over a gentle heat. Add the water, which should cover the vegetables, and cook for a further 15 minutes. Remove from the heat and add the herbs. After 5 minutes strain and reduce the stock by about half. Season lightly.

Yields 500 ml

50 g butter
2 courgettes, roughly chopped
2 leeks, roughly chopped
2 carrots, peeled and roughly chopped
2 celery sticks, unpeeled, roughly chopped
5 cloves garlic, peeled and crushed
1 fennel bulb, roughly chopped
1 onion, roughly chopped
1½ litres water
1 tablespoon basil, fresh
1 tablespoon tarragon, fresh
salt and freshly ground black pepper

Flavoured Oils

Basil Oil

Method

Purée the basil with a little cold water (about 1–2 tablespoons). Do this quickly, as if you process the basil for too long, it can react with the metal on the blade and lose its bright colour. Transfer to a bowl and gradually whisk in the oil. Season and add the garlic. Refrigerate for up to 3 days.

100 g basil
200 ml olive oil
salt and freshly ground black pepper
2 cloves garlic, peeled

Beetroot Oil

Method

This is only practical to make when you are cooking beetroot.

Cook the beetroot in boiling salted water and then drain. Reserve the juice, and place in a saucepan with the balsamic vinegar and sugar. Reduce by half, and then whisk with the olive oil. Season and refrigerate for up to 2–3 days.

4 beetroot
2 tablespoons balsamic vinegar
1 teaspoon sugar
100 ml olive oil
salt and pepper

Dill Oil

Method

Mix all the ingredients together and store for 2–3 days in the refrigerator.

100 g dill, finely chopped
200 ml olive oil
salt and freshly ground black pepper
juice of 1 lemon

Curry Oil

Method

Preheat the oven to 150°C/300°F/gas mark 2.
Place all the ingredients (except the olive oil) on a roasting tray. Pour 100 ml oil over, and roast for an hour. Transfer the ingredients into a medium saucepan along with the remaining oil. Cook over a very gentle heat for 2 hours. Remove from the heat, cool overnight and then strain. Store refrigerated for 2–3 days.

2 cloves garlic, peeled and roughly chopped
2 shallots, peeled and roughly chopped
2 sprigs thyme
3 tablespoons curry powder
1 teaspoon cumin
1 teaspoon fennel seeds, crushed
salt and freshly ground black pepper
300 ml olive oil

Chive Oil

Chive oil is a great accompaniment to salads, grilled vegetables, fish and chicken. We make the chive paste in the food processor, but we whisk in the remaining oil by hand, as the oil tends to lose some of its colour when overprocessed.

Method
Blanch the chives in boiling salted water for approximately 5 seconds and immediately refresh under cold running water. Pat dry with kitchen paper and then chop roughly.

Place the chives in a food processor together with the garlic, basil, pepper and a tablespoon of water. Blend until you have a smooth paste.

Transfer the mixture to a large bowl. Gradually whisk in the olive oil by hand and then adjust the seasoning. Store for 2–3 days in the refrigerator.
Note: We make the chive paste in the food processor, but we whisk in the remaining oil by hand, as the oil tends to lose some of its colour when overprocessed.

100 g fresh chives
salt
1 clove garlic, peeled and crushed
1 tablespoon basil, chopped
freshly ground black pepper
200 ml olive oil

Tomato Oil

Heat a tablespoon of olive oil in a medium-sized saucepan and add the garlic, shallots, celery, fennel, basil, oregano and bay leaves. Sweat together for 5 minutes until the vegetables are tender, but do not allow to colour. Add the tomato pureé and mix well.

Continue to cook gently for another 10 minutes, making sure the heat is very low, as the mixture is quite dry and could burn easily. Gradually add the remaining oil, stirring continuously. Season well and cook gently for another 1½–2 hours.

Allow to cool and pass the mixture through a fine sieve; the oil will have separated from the sediment. For an extra-clear oil, strain twice through muslin. Adjust seasoning if necessary. Store for 2–3 days in the refrigerator.

200 ml olive oil
2 cloves garlic, peeled and crushed
2 shallots, peeled and chopped
1 celery stick, chopped
¼ fennel bulb, chopped
1 tablespoon basil, chopped
½ tablespoon oregano, chopped
2 bay leaves
40 ml tomato pureé
salt and freshly ground black pepper

Vinaigrettes

Lemon Grass Vinaigrette

Method

Bruise the lemon grass using a rolling pin or the bottom of a saucepan. Place the olive oil in a small saucepan with the lemon grass and heat through for a minute. Leave to infuse for 15 minutes.

Mix together the tarragon vinegar, sugar, salt and pepper. Remove the lemon grass from the olive oil and discard. Gradually whisk the olive oil into the tarragon vinegar. Refrigerate until ready to use.

Serves 4

1 stalk lemon grass
150 ml olive oil
50 ml tarragon vinegar
1 teaspoon sugar
salt and freshly ground pepper

Ginger and Basil Vinaigrette

The earlier you make this the better, as the flavours will have more time to develop. The egg yolk gives the dressing an added richness, but is not vital to the recipe.

Method

Place all the ingredients in a blender or food processor and blend until smooth. Refrigerate until ready to use. Use within 24 hours.

Serves 4

110 ml olive oil
30 ml balsamic vinegar
1 shallot, peeled and roughly chopped
1 clove garlic, peeled and crushed
1 tablespoon basil leaves
2.5 cm piece root ginger, peeled and finely chopped
1 teaspoon sugar
2 tablespoons warm water
1 egg yolk (optional)
salt and freshly ground black pepper

Truffle Vinaigrette

Method

Whisk the first 5 ingredients together. Allow the flavours to develop for a few hours and just before serving mix in the tomato and chives. Season and serve immediately.

Serves 4

110 ml olive oil
30 ml balsamic vinaigrette
1 teaspoon sugar
1 tablespoon truffle trimmings
1 teaspoon truffle oil
1 tomato, skinned, seeded and finely diced
1 small bunch chives, finely chopped
salt and freshly ground black pepper

Balsamic Vinaigrette

We make our vinaigrette using a very good quality balsamic vinegar, preferably a twelve-year-old, and the best extra virgin olive oil we can buy. With other varieties of salad dressings such as Caesar dressing, you don't have to use olive oils and vinegars of the same standard, as they usually contain so many ingredients that the virtues of a beautiful twelve-year-old balsamic go unnoticed.

Vinegar is made by fermenting red or white wine, sherry or cider. Balsamic vinegar is made from Italian red wine that undergoes a laborious fermentation process. Aceto Balsamico Tradizionale is made in Modena and Emilia and is so valued that supply can hardly keep up with demand.

Only vinegars of the highest quality gain official designation from the Italian government. They must be aged for a minimum of 12 years. Approved vinegars are usually those that have been aged for 20–30 years and have been tested by an official board of tasters. The vinegars that reach this status are few, and are used sparingly. They are usually thick, rich and syrup-like and are sometimes drunk like a liqueur. They sell for hundreds of pounds and must not be mistaken for the majority of 'balsamic vinegars' available on the market.

Method

Place all the ingredients in a blender or food processor and blend until smooth.

Refrigerate until ready to use. Use within 3 or 4 days.

Serves 4
110 ml olive oil
30 ml good quality balsamic vinegar
½ shallot, peeled and roughly chopped
½ teaspoon sugar
salt and freshly ground black pepper

nutrients escaping from the vegetables. Salted water has a higher temperature when boiling than unsalted water so vegetables cook quicker.

Fry or pan fry: cook over a high heat allowing the food to gain plenty of colour.

Poach: cook in liquid over a very gentle heat. Food that is poached should not obtain any colour.

Roast: this term often conjures up images of roast beef but in the restaurant world it is loosely used to describe food that has been subjected to intense heat. A dish called roasted monkfish has probably been seared and then basted in butter, madeira and rosemary and finished in a very hot oven.

Sauté: cook over a high heat, allowing the food to colour.

Sear: cook meat in fat over a very high heat to give maximum colour and to lock in moisture. We always sear fish, chicken or game skin side down first, as it makes the skin taste much better and appear more appetising. When searing meat you sometimes find that it's hard to turn the meat over, as it sticks to the pan. This is because when the meat hits the pan the blood rushes to the pan's surface and sticks to it. After a minute or so it will release itself naturally, so don't force it.

Fat
To get rid of excess fat in meat or game, for example, mince or duck, blanch it for a few minutes.

If you want to cut down on the amount of butter or cream in a recipe reduce the quantity but do not substitute low fat alternatives. These, together with low sodium salt and artificial sweeteners give an unpleasant flavour to food and cannot replace the real thing.

Fish
Whole fresh fish should feel quite slippery and the flesh should be firm. It should not have a strong fishy smell.

Herbs
Always use fresh herbs unless otherwise stated.

Hollandaise sauce
How to save it when you run into problems *see* Aïoli.

Ingredients
We always use the freshest and best ingredients we can possibly buy and have that advantage over home cooks as our ingredients are delivered daily to the restaurant. Do try to ensure that your ingredients are as fresh as possible.

Julienne strips
Very fine matchsticks-size strips of vegetables.

Ketaifi dough is shredded filo pastry. It is available in specialist shops.

Lobsters

The reason lobsters should always be bought live is that their diet is full of toxins which means that when the lobster dies the flesh is liable to go off rapidly. If you don't like the thought of killing the lobster buy cooked lobster meat from a good fishmonger.

Mise en place

This is what we refer to when describing our 'prep' work. The mise en place for each section (the starter section, the fish section, the meat section, etc.) of the kitchen starts first thing each day. Making stocks, sauces and dressings, preparing, trimming and filleting meat and fish, preparing and chopping vegetables—these are just a few of the chores chefs do each day. When you are making these dishes at home, you will do a certain amount of mise en place for each dish, whether it be making a salad dressing, or a purée to eventually add to a risotto, or pin-boning and chilling salmon. It is all about being organised and prepared, and allows you to cook in a more confident style.

Olive oil

We always use olive oil when cooking, except for deep fat frying when we use vegetable oil. We use extra virgin olive oil only when making dressings because when the oil is subjected to intense heat it loses some of its chemical properties.

Onions/Shallots

Depending on the recipe, onions are sometimes allowed to take on colour. When they are not to take on colour, it is usually because we want to keep the colour in a dish very pale, and bring out the natural sweetness without getting a caramelised taste.

Parmesan

Parmesan is easier to grate if first placed in the freezer for 10 minutes. Use a vegetable peeler to make shavings.

Quenelles

In the restaurant world, the term quenelle is used to describe a shape (three-sided oval) rather than its technical meaning which is fish or white meat, bound with cream and eggs and gently poached.

Refresh

To refresh is to cool ingredients quickly either under running water, or plunged into ice cold water. This stops the cooking process immediately, crisps up vegetables and sets the colour.

Seasoning

Always use a good quality sea salt, and freshly ground black or white pepper.

Stock

Good chefs treat their stock pots with loving care as they are fully aware of the benefits of a good stock. However, cooking in a restaurant is a full time occupation and few of us at home have the time to make stock. It is perfectly acceptable for home cooks to use stock cubes with the addition of a few herbs. When we were testing the recipes we sometimes used water, not stock, and the dishes still tasted superb. The flavour would only be enhanced further by the use of stock. So please do not be put off a recipe when you see the word 'stock' as you may find yourself limited in what you can cook.

If you want to freeze stock, reduce it first by rapid boiling until it's very thick and jelly-like. Allow it to cool and then freeze in small containers. When you need to use the stock, remove the amount you need from the freezer, add enough water to give a well-flavoured stock, and heat thoroughly.

Sugar

Always use white sugar unless demerara is specified. Always use caster sugar except when making caramel, when you should use granulated sugar.

Tomatoes

How to skin and deseed: cut out the eye from the top of the tomato. Drop it into a saucepan of boiling water for 10 seconds, then remove it with a slotted spoon and place in a bowl of cold water. The skin should peel away when gently pulled. If it doesn't come away easily, return the tomato to the boiling water for a few more seconds and then refresh again in the cold water. The skin should now peel away easily. Cut the tomatoes in half horizontally and use a teaspoon to scoop out the seeds.

Tomato purée

It's a good idea to heat tomato purée in a small saucepan before using as it helps to get rid of the 'tinned' taste.

Vegetables

Always wash and dry vegetables before using. The only exceptions are mushrooms which absorb far too much liquid and should therefore be wiped with a damp cloth instead.

To turn: using a 'turning' knife, shape vegetables into small barrel shapes. Initially practise on soft vegetables such as courgettes, and then work on carrots and turnips.

North American equivalent terms

aubergine/eggplant

bacon rashers/bacon slices

beetroot/beet

caster sugar/super fine sugar

chicory/Belgian endive

clingfilm/plastic wrap

coriander (dried)/coriander

coriander (leaf)/cilantro

cos/romaine

courgette/zucchini

curly endive/chicory

essence/extract

frying pan/skillet

icing sugar/confectioner's sugar

langoustine/lobster tail

muslin/cheesecloth

natural yoghurt/plain yoghurt

oven ready chicken/broiler/fryer

Parma ham/prosciutto

pickling onions/pearl onions

pigeon/squab

pip/seed

plain flour/all purpose flour

plain/dark chocolate/semi-sweet chocolate

poussin/rock cornish hen

prawns/shrimp

Puy lentils/French green lentils

rocket/arugula

scampi/jumbo shrimp

shortcrust pastry/pie dough

spring onions/scallions/green onions

stone/pit

sultanas/golden raisins

to grill/to broil

treacle/molasses

wholemeal flour/wholewheat flour

Conversion Chart

In the recipes we give the measurements in metric. However, except for the pastries, slightly inaccurate quantities will not make any noticeable difference to the end result.

Dry measures

15 g	½ oz	1 tablespoon
100 g	4 oz	½ cup/1 stick
225 g	8 oz	1 cup/2 sticks

Liquid measures

15 ml	½ fl oz	1 tablespoon
50 ml	2 fl oz	¼ cup
100 ml	4 fl oz	½ cup
225 ml	8 fl oz	1 cup
300 ml	½ pint	1¼ cups
600 ml	1 pint	2½ cups

Specialist Suppliers

The following companies are all experts in their respective fields. We have found them to be excellent suppliers of specialist products that we regularly use in Peacock Alley.

IRELAND

Wines, Spirits and Beverages
New Age Beverages
Clondalkin
Dublin 22
Distributors of EVIAN Natural Mineral Water

Findlaters (Wine Merchants) Ltd
The Harcourt Street Vaults
10 Upper Hatch Street
Dublin 2

Gilbey's Wine and Spirits Merchants
Gilbey House
Belgard Road
Dublin 24

Grants of Ireland
St Laurence Road
Chapelizod
Dublin 20

James Nicholson Wine Merchant
27A Killyleagh
Crossgar
Co. Down BT30 9DQ

Remy Ireland Ltd
101 Monkstown Road
Monkstown
Co Dublin

Wines Direct
Lisamate
Irishtown
Mullingar
Co Westmeath

Hamboven Sales Ltd
Willow House
1–2 Cross Avenue
Dun Laoghaire
Co Dublin
The home of famous coffee such as IDEE and Alfredo.

Kitchen Equipment
Kaneco Ltd.
Unit 76
Western Parkway Business Park
Ballymount Road
Dublin 12
For excellent design and layout of restaurant kitchens, and suppliers of many world famous brands of coffee and espresso machines, refrigeration and other kitchen equipment such as La Cimbali and Ambach.

Sweeney & O'Rourke
34 Pearse Stret
Dublin 2
Catering sundryware, trolleys, kitchen equipment and knives.

Dairy Products
G & C Power
68 Whitechurch Way
Ballyboden
Dublin 16

Fruit, Vegetables and Herbs
Glendawn Country Fresh Herbs
1a Little Green Street
Dublin 7
Specialising in fresh herbs and lettuces.

Frank Newman
Fruit and Vegetable Wholesaler
27 Camden Street
Dublin 2

Harmons Wholesale and Retail
Greengrocers
9 Moreen Walk
Sandyford
Dublin 16

Here Today
25 South Anne Street
Dublin 2

Dry Goods and Fine Foods

La Rousse Foods
73 Western Parkway Business Park
Lower Ballymount Road
Dublin 12
Specialising in many imported products
and fine foods from France including ketaifi
dough and pistachio paste.

BW Marketing
Crag
Torca Road
Dalkey
Co Dublin
Agents for Crismona extra virgin olive oils
and other fine foods including saffron,
herbs, spices, Williamson and Magor Fine
Teas.

Elliots
4–10 Camden Row
Dublin 8

Meat, Fish and Poultry

Wrights of Howth
West Pier
Howth
Co Dublin
Wholesale fish and poultry products.

M & B Butchers
639 South Circular Road
Kilmainham
Dublin 8
Wholesale and retail suppliers of beef, lamb,
pork and bacon.

M & K Butchers
Main Street
Tallaght Village
Dublin 24
Specialising in wholesale and retail meat,
poultry and game.

Maree Oysters Ltd
Aphouleen
Maree
Clarinbridge
Co Galway

Miscellaneous

The Decent Cigar Company
46 Grafton Street
Dublin 2
Ireland's leading supplier of premium hand
rolled cigars and accessories.

Creative Works Ltd
59 Ramleh Park
Milltown
Dublin 6
A unique menu design and production
workshop offering a combination of
creativity and flexibility in culinary
presentation.

Glenmore Linens
Cappry
Ballybofey
Co Donegal
Suppliers of all textile requirements for
restaurants, hotels, etc.

NEW YORK

Irish Food Distributors
500 Saw Mill River Road
Yonkers
New York 10701
USA
Specialist importers of Irish products into
the USA, such as butter, cheese, bacon,
black pudding, chocolate and salmon.

INDEX